What L

WHAT DOESN'T KILL YOU

Fifteen Stories of Survival

Edited by Elitsa Dermendzhiyska

unbound

First published in 2020

Unbound
6th Floor Mutual House, 70 Conduit Street, London W1S 2GF

www.unbound.com

Text design by Ellipsis, Glasgow

A CIP record for this book is available from the British Library

ISBN 978-1-78352-764-9 (trade pbk)
ISBN 978-1-78352-778-6 (ebook)
ISBN 978-1-78352-725-0 (limited edition)

Printed and bound in Great Britain by Clays Ltd, Elcograf S.p.A.

What Doesn't Kill You is published with thanks for support from a number of patrons:

KPMG

MediaCom

Dr Frederick Mulder CBE

Pets at Home

Sage

The best way to educate, challenge opinion and remove stigma is to articulate experience through storytelling and personal experience. It is only through hearing the impact on an individual that you can truly start to empathise and challenge your own views. Education and the removal of stigma around mental health has, and continues to be, a key focus for The Ardonagh Group and we've made great strides in this area – with more progress still to be made. We are proud to have supported *What Doesn't Kill You* and helped to share such impactful stories around this important issue.

The Ardonagh Group

I have had a good fifty-year career in the drinks industry, but in 2016, due to severe stress, I had major mental health issues. When I recovered, I decided to give back to society in this crucial arena and am now President of The Shaw Mind Foundation: www.shawmindfoundation.org. Our mission is to provide society and communities with mental health and wellbeing support.

Dr James Espey OBE

You never know what other people are going through. Over the years, I've employed over 4,000 people and I learned very quickly that lots of them live with secret battles every day. So, I made it my business to ensure that staff and their families were supported and that they had full access to employee assistance programmes. Since selling my company, I still feel a huge sense of loyalty to my team and will continue to support projects that promote mental wellness.

Helen McArdle CBE, entrepreneur and philanthropist

We are the leading Microsoft Dynamics NAV and Dynamics 365 Business Central reseller in the UK. We're slightly quirkier than the average software reseller and have a very passionate, innovative and customer-centric company culture. As a company we provide staff with the necessary means to support their mental health and have a team of volunteers available to give advice and help those in need.

The NAV | 365 People

Onfido is a proud sponsor of *What Doesn't Kill You*. It is incumbent on businesses, as a key pillar of society, to respond to the mental health challenges of the modern world by supporting employees to bring their whole being to work – during bad times as well as good. We try our best to make this a reality in our culture and practices, as it is simply the right and moral thing to do. Happily, what is good for human beings is almost always good for business too!

Onfido

London-based tech firm Softwire has spent the last twenty years building the best environment for its staff to thrive. We think commercial pressures should sit alongside human ones: that putting staff welfare first also makes us more successful. Our efforts to make that a reality include launching a discussion around mental health. We're still figuring some things out, but just like maintaining code, it's not about being perfect – it's about continuously questioning and having the courage to change.

Softwire

Founders of start-ups face both common and unique stressors that can trigger mental wellness challenges. At Techstars, we believe it's important to support founders by having open and honest conversations about mental wellness. Within our accelerator programs specifically, we encourage self-care and activities to help develop positive mental wellness habits and successful approaches to managing stress.

Brad Feld, Techstars co-founder

Contents

III. Striving

Foreword

In 2016 I left my job as product manager of the technology start-up I'd co-founded in London and set out to study mental health. Over the next year I dug into psychology, neuroscience and genetics, interviewed clinicians, nurses and psycho-therapists, talked to entrepreneurs, City professionals, video-game players, artists and young people. The more I learned, the more enamoured I became of our shared human experience – from the tenderness of our pain to the exquisite resilience that runs through us even when we are at our most fragile. Never before had I heard more fascinating stories – not in the public conversations about mental health, not even in the books I devoured in a desperate search for insight.

And so I decided to create the book which I wanted to read but could not find. The idea was simple: to seek out the most original thinkers in the UK who were willing to reveal their deepest personal struggles on the page. Months of detective work, aided by a blissful ignorance of book publishing, finally yielded the beguiling cast of characters you'll meet in this book. They include acclaimed novelists, beloved comedians, ingenious artists, distinguished academics and trailblazing explorers who will take you on a journey to the darkest recesses of their minds. And as they probe their most private fears, the authors will grapple with questions that haunt all of us:

How can we live with our demons?
How can we grow from our wounds?
How can we write another story when the one we wanted is taken away from us?

Despite its heavy subject matter, this is a hopeful book. Its hope, however, is not the cheap kind peddled by the masters of self-help. It's the kind of hope you can only find when you let the old delusions go and learn to dance with your fears.

Elitsa Dermendzhiyska
London, April 2019

I. Struggle

Beginning

David Whyte

Poet David Whyte grew up with a strong, imaginative influence from his Irish mother among the hills and valleys of his father's Yorkshire. The author of nine books of poetry and four books of prose, he now lives in the Pacific Northwest of the United States.

Beginning well or beginning poorly, what is important is simply to begin, but the ability to make a good beginning is also an art form. Beginning well involves a clearing away of the crass, the irrelevant and the complicated to find the beautiful, often hidden lineaments of the essential and the necessary.

Beginning is difficult, and our procrastination is a fine ever-present measure of our reluctance in taking that first close-in, courageous step to reclaiming our happiness. Perhaps, because taking a new step always leads to a kind of radical internal simplification, where, suddenly, very large parts of us, parts of us we have kept gainfully employed for years, parts of us still rehearsing the old complicated story, are suddenly out of a job.

There occurs, in effect, a form of internal corporate down-sizing, where the parts of us too afraid to participate or having nothing now to offer are let go, with all of the accompanying death-like trauma, and where the very last fight occurs, a rear-guard disbelief that this new, less complicated self, and this very simple step, is all that is needed for the new possibilities ahead.

It is always hard to believe that the courageous step is so close to us, that it is closer than we ever could imagine, that in fact, we already know what it is, and that the step is simpler, more radical than we had thought: which is why we so often prefer the story to be more elaborate, our identities clouded by fear, the horizon safely in the distance, the essay longer than it needs to be and the answer safely in the realm of impossibility.

Eight

A. J. Ashworth

A. J. Ashworth is the author of the prize-winning short story collection Somewhere Else, or Even Here *and the editor of* Red Room: New Short Stories Inspired by the Brontës. *She lives with her family in Blackburn, plays online chess (badly), and likes astronomy and dragonflies.*

Everything is the past.

It is all around us, inside us. In our blood, in our bones, in our memories. It endures. Like a cockroach that survives a nuclear bomb. It is everything and everywhere. It is even in the light that we see – because of that distance between object and eye. The past is never the past. It is here. And here. And here. It lives. The past is our present. It is our now.

I. WHEN WE LOOK AT THE SUN, WE ARE SEEING EIGHT MINUTES INTO THE PAST

This is how I want to begin this – with the first of eight things I know about the sun. None of them is anything much to do

5

with what I want to write about, not really, and yet they are. Or they can be. Either way, I need these eight things to give shape to what I want to say, to give form to what is formless ... to have control over my story.

Perhaps this is part of the problem: the wanting of control.

There is sun – I think – the first time it happens. Out in the back garden of my parents' house when I am eight. Climbing up onto the roof of the shed – in the same way my friends have just done a few minutes before.

I do not know then that the sunlight that illuminates everything around me is ancient light, is light that has taken eight minutes to travel the 93 million miles across space between sun and earth. And before that, thousands of years to escape the hot grasp of our parent star. I do not know what causes the sunlight to seem strange as I finally talk myself into jumping that small distance between roof and grass. I just know that after I land I feel off-kilter, untethered, too loose inside my head – like a sail with a rope cut. Is it that old light that has changed or something in me?

But even then I know.

It is not the light.

There has been some tilting in my perception; some change that has come from doing something I haven't done before; a mental rebellion.

I can still hear the words I shout as I get up from the grass and run into the house to try and escape that strange light, that spacey feeling of being offset from myself.

'I'm going to die!'

Running for the stairs. Massaging my temples to stop the sensations. Feeling that I am on the verge of being swatted out of life.

My mum standing, on the phone to someone, and turning as I run past. 'What?'

'I'm going to die!'

'What do you . . . ?'

'I'M GOING TO DIE!'

Even now, I can still see the grass and the light and my mum's back as she talks on the phone. I can still remember the feel of panic in my veins: the cold drain of it, like a sluicing within.

And even though it is the first time those feelings come, it won't be the last. Perhaps I even knew that then.

2. IF THE SUN WERE TO DISAPPEAR, IT WOULD TAKE EIGHT MINUTES FOR DARKNESS TO FALL

There was a me before that point and a me after, as if that first panic attack somehow caused a shearing in the once-solid iceberg of me.

I had always been a sensitive child – all blush and hide. But that sudden, overwhelming feeling of terror, the light-headedness, the fastness of my heart was new, had come out of nowhere. And because I didn't understand it, it made me worry that it might happen again. Which of course it did.

'What are you doing?'

'Nothing.'

'Try and get to sleep, love.'

I am about ten. It is the early hours of the morning. I am at the home for the elderly where my mum sometimes works in the office. She is sleeping in for the night and I am staying with her. More than once, there has been talk of ghosts among the staff, about Ouija boards, about the care assistant who is psychic, who was once manhandled by a spirit, whose face sometimes changes into that of her Chinese spirit guide – all subjects that I, with my love of the supernatural, like to hear about. But now, in the darkness, in the supposedly haunted flat that is part of the home, my heart is racing and the feelings of unreality are back. I am worried that if I sleep I will be open to these strange forces, that I will become possessed, lose myself. I am worried that my boundaries will be too easily crossed.

I roll onto my front and prop myself up, stare at my mum's mouth to check she's still breathing. She is. I try to match my breathing to hers. She opens her eyes and studies my face, knots of worry in her forehead.

'What are you doing?'

'Nothing.'

I can't tell her what's happening, can't admit that I am terrified down to my marrow. It would make things too real, make everything worse. I'm not sure where this thought comes from, but for some reason I believe it would lead to me losing control or going mad. It is better for me – I think – to try and pretend I'm OK, to hope nobody notices, to just push the feelings away. But it is like trying to fight the pull of gravity.

I lie back down and try to breathe my heart towards slowness. But it carries on thumping. My head continues to feel tilted and wrong inside. I close my eyes and will away the demon that might want to get inside me. I try to sleep but I'm not sure that I do. I just want the morning light to come, to take the dark stain of night away and save me. That is what I want more than anything.

3. THE SUN SPINS FASTER AT ITS EQUATOR

Some of these don't seem to fit as easily as others. But I've chosen the sun for a reason – because of the symbolism of light and dark, because of how sunlight means the past, because of how I orbit panic in the same way we orbit the sun; at least that's what I tell myself. And there are words – there in each fact and then mirrored in what follows: eight, darkness, spins … None of this is random. There is meaning here, there is craft. I tell you to show you that I'm in control of this. I tell you in the hope that you will help in making meaning out of this.

Eventually sunlight *does* arrive after the night. But it doesn't take away my dark, which is too far inside me to reach now. Like a black bulb buried deep that I cannot find the switch for. I carry it with me everywhere, without anyone else knowing. All through my childhood it will come on whenever it likes, when I least expect it – when sitting and watching something lighthearted on TV, when playing card games with my grandparents, when eating an ice cream I've been asking for but then have to abandon because I'm unable to eat when I feel like this.

This thing I do not understand punctuates my life, some-times draining the light out of my days. It refuses to go even when adulthood comes, even when I know what it is and can speak its name. But panic is not Rumpelstiltskin, whose power leaves him when the girl who spins gold learns what he's called. It is no fairy tale, no matter how much I might have wished it was. Still might wish it to be.

4. THE AMOUNT OF SUNLIGHT HITTING THE SURFACE OF THE EARTH IS KNOWN AS SOLAR INTENSITY

'Why are you upset? You're young, you should be happy.'

This is what the doctor tells me, with kindness, with a smile – the doctor who has known me since birth, who has seen me through bouts of tonsillitis and earache and is now witnessing me, in my twenties, having a breakdown.

'I know,' I say. 'I know.' He gives me a prescription for anti-depressants.

'Try and relax,' he says before he leaves, and he's right, of course he is. But my brain has forgotten what it is to relax. It has lost the ability to summon ease and so I am unable to feel it.

I am off work, at home in my pyjamas, in a state of acute anxiety; unable to eat because of extreme nausea, hardly sleeping, crying, not washing or having baths – even the thought of turning on the kettle is too much to bear. Two weeks in and I have lost over a stone in weight and become agoraphobic. And I don't even know what has caused it. A minor fallout is the only thing slightly out of the ordinary that has happened. But it isn't that. It is nothing more than perhaps a feeling of vulnerability and a fleeting worry or two – but these are just the extra little straws on top of a lifetime of them that my camel cannot carry. They are enough for the punch of panic to come to my stomach and for the anxiety to take hold in a way it hasn't before; the intensity enough to make me vomit – which I do in my bedroom bin, because I cannot make it to the bathroom.

It is after days of this, when I am pale and thin as a candle, that my parents call the doctor and he comes with his prescription – to the house because I can't even get into the surgery. And that night, unable to sleep, I take one of his pills. But because I then worry about taking them, about relying on such things – which makes me feel even more on edge – I throw them in the bin.

Out of despair I phone the Samaritans. They ask me if I want to take my own life. I don't. I just want to feel normal again, I say. When I realise they won't be able to help me, I decide to say goodbye and hang up. I had hoped that talking to them, off-loading to a stranger, would help somehow but it doesn't.

I don't know what to do. There are no instructions for finding a way out of the woods of this. It – this anxiety, this panic – has me. I have to accept that. It has me for as long as it wants me.

5. SUNSPOTS ARE COOLER REGIONS ON THE SUN'S SURFACE AND CAN LAST FOR DAYS OR EVEN MONTHS

'Here,' my then boyfriend says, sunlight spearing in through a gap in the curtains. 'Eat a bit at least.'

It is a few days after the doctor's visit. But I am no longer at home. I am in Bristol at his grandparents' farmhouse, where he is living while at university. He has brought me down from Blackburn so that I can stay here while they're away on holiday. 'Maybe you just need some time away,' he'd said. 'Peace and quiet.' He'd driven 200 miles to collect me, making the return journey in the dark, with me barely speaking beside him because I felt so low.

It is the morning after he picked me up now and he is sitting on the edge of the bed with a single piece of toast on a plate, offering it to me; my stomach knotted with nausea at the thought of putting it in my mouth. But I know he's right and that I should force myself. I take the plate from him and nibble at a corner of the toast, concentrating hard to make myself swallow a couple of pieces. I manage but then have to stop and give the plate back to him.

'Try a bit more,' he says.

But I can't. The nausea has won and I'm unable to swallow anything else.

Worrying about not eating doesn't help: if this carries on there's a chance I might starve to death. This is what my brain keeps telling me, making my stomach tighten even more. 'I'm going to die,' I said during my first panic attack as a child – and now I feel I might be proved right.

My boyfriend is dark beneath his eyes from the stress of all this – same as my parents. I would like nothing more than to eat and be well for all of them, be happy as I should be – but

I can't. The black bulb is refusing to go out. It is shining dark and strong, robust as a cockroach.

He stands with the plate, pulls at the curtains until the sun bursts through fully, making me frown and blink at its brightness. There are white sunspots behind my eyes from the intensity of the light. 'We'll try again soon.'

I nod, even though eating is the last thing I seem able to do. But I nod anyway. I want to eat. I want to be rid of this dread and sadness. I want to be well.

6. THE SUN GOES THROUGH BOTH ACTIVE AND QUIET PHASES

Eventually I do start to eat – a little, then a little more. Quiet time on my own helps. This cottage is still as a stopped clock. It gives me a feeling of almost existing outside of time: in the bardo, neither one place nor another. Perhaps it is just what I need.

Being in nature helps too – I go outside and chop wood for the fire, the sun and breeze on my face as I aim, swing high; I love the sound of the axe hitting the log, how the pale insides of the pieces of split wood tumble to the side like lovers. I come back inside with armfuls, load up the wood burner, light the kindling and wait for the flames to take hold. Sometimes, I just sit and watch them, basking in the heat and the sounds of the crackling logs. Sometimes I read, and the words and the warmth soothe me towards a peacefulness I haven't felt in weeks.

The quiet, chopping wood, being soft and slow in the world – it all helps. And gradually I begin to return to myself, although it will be months before the aftershocks of this particular earthquake reduce to levels no louder than the usual noise of anxiety. But the crisis has passed. I am out of the bardo and back in the world again. I am returned, although a little changed.

7. THE SUN'S ATMOSPHERE IS MADE UP OF THE PHOTOSPHERE, THE CHROMOSPHERE AND THE CORONA

There are other facts about the sun I could choose – but somehow these are the ones that come. I could talk about how over a million earths can fit inside it, how it contains 99.9 per cent of the mass of the solar system, how it has a solar wind that streams out into the blackness, but for some reason these aren't right. So instead, I talk about sunspots, the speed of light, the atmosphere. All the while hoping that all of this is making sense.

Where do you go when you cannot escape yourself?

I am on holiday with my boyfriend, a different one – in a place I haven't been before: Mallorca. Hardly exotic or challenging or wildly different from home. And yet here I am, throwing up in the toilet while the old sun bakes and yellows the landscape. It is meant to be a break away from work, a chance to relax, but instead my brain has decided that this place is some kind of threat to me. And so my body is making itself lighter – ready for the fight or flight that comes from fear: our programmed and ancient animal response to danger. Only there is nothing to run from, nowhere to run to – especially when the predator and the prey are both inside me.

There is the fast heartbeat, the light-headedness, the feeling of dread – the worry that I will not be able to cope, that another breakdown will happen. And once that first worrying thought comes, the rest grow like bacteria in a petri dish. It is almost impossible to stop the spread of them.

What has started things this time – I think – as with all my panic episodes, is a hypersensitivity to my internal atmosphere, an awareness of some change somewhere inside, perhaps a flickering of fear in my gut, a light-headedness caused by thoughts of being somewhere unknown, where I can't get back home easily. There is worry that I won't be able to just crawl into bed until this passes, that if the panic takes hold, I will stop eating again, and what then? And there is also the extra pressure I put on myself. What if my new boyfriend thinks I'm mad, wants to get rid? We're on holiday, we're meant to be having a good time, we should be eating nice food and sightseeing. I should be functioning like a normal person. But all this, somehow, is too much. It is too much to come on holiday and enjoy myself. And so the fear and vomiting begin.

It takes a few days of not eating, not feeling right, before the panic subsides. But the connection has been made now: holidays = anxiety/panic. And so when we go to Canada some years later, on a trip we have both dreamed of, to celebrate the end of our master's degrees, it happens again. Only this time it's worse – I'm further away from home than I've ever been. I can't get back easily. There is the squirm of fear in my belly, the speeding heartbeat, the feeling of losing control. I lie on the bed of our hotel room after we arrive and feel dizzy, nauseous. My boyfriend wants to go for a meal but I can't eat, can't leave the room. I tell him to go and get something, knowing that I'm ruining this dream holiday of ours. The look in his eyes tells me I'm right.

I force myself to go downstairs to the restaurant with him but I can't order anything. I sit and watch him eat, battling with myself to lighten up, enjoy this, chill out. But nothing works. At night, I go to bed but don't sleep. My heart races and I still feel light-headed, worry that I'm going to go mad, have a breakdown, die from not eating for two weeks. I come to the conclusion I will have to go home. There is nothing else for it but to go to the airport and get on the next plane back.

I talk to him in the morning and cry about it. He asks me why I'm letting it control me, why I'm letting it win. For a day or so I'm hurt that he doesn't seem to understand this. But then I wonder if he's right – if all I need to do is to get some power back over it.

I take a pillow from the bed and push my face into it. 'You fucking fucker, fuck off and leave me alone! You're not fucking ruining my life!' I scream into the clean, white bulk of it. And then I scream some more. 'Just fucking get fucked!' I lift the pillow and punch it as if it's a face. 'Fuck off, why don't you? Just fuck off!' Punch, punch, punch. And then I throw the pillow back onto the bed.

Something about this makes me feel lighter. The nausea and the light-headedness and the fast heartbeat are all still there, but there is a feeling of lift too – the possibility of being free of this, for now at least.

The morning after, I manage to go out, take a bus ride to Niagara Falls, put on a poncho and get in a boat, *The Maid of the Mist*. The panic is subsiding a little. I can sense it. I breathe in deep, soak in the sight of hundreds of rainbows caused by the mist thrown up into the air from the force of the Horseshoe Falls. I blink at the brightness of the sunlight reflected from all the water droplets. I am drenched in spray, childlike in the joy of it. Today is a good day. A very good day. There is sunlight and rainbows – almost a fairy-tale ending. Only there is no ending. Not really. There's only ever a going on.

8. THE SUN IS ABOUT HALFWAY THROUGH ITS LIFE – THE MIDPOINT BETWEEN BIRTH AND DEATH

The sun – our wonderful, average star – is middle-aged now, at the midpoint between birth and death. Same as me. When it reaches the end of its life, it will use up the final remnants of its fuel and expand out into the solar system to form a red giant – swallowing up the inner planets as its outer shell grows, then possibly earth, possibly. But the end won't really be the end for the sun. Nothing will be lost. Its elements will be cast out into the universe to form new stars, new solar systems. We will just have to wait 5 billion years to see what happens, see what kind of planetary nebula it will make in the night sky. However it looks in the end, it will be a beautiful burst of colourful dust and gas that hopefully will be visible to somebody somewhere. In some not-too-distant galaxy. Old, beautiful light that will continue to travel in all directions forever more.

As I type this, there is light hitting me from the computer screen that is nanoseconds old. It is new light really, in the scheme of things. But still, it is light that shows me the past – even if only nanoseconds into the past. I see the computer as it was, not as it is. It's still hard to grasp, at times, the notion that light travels. But it is what we have come to understand: photons journey through time and space, and each is the memory of where it began.

I'm going to switch this computer off soon – shut down its man-made light – and go instead to the window, or maybe outside. To where that old sunlight is streaming down, to where it will shower me in the ancient photons formed from the violent collisions of atoms at the heart of the sun. I am calm today, calmer this year than I've ever been. But I don't have any answers as to why. I just am and so I accept it. I welcome it. I hope that it continues.

There *are* things I do, though, to try to keep fear at bay. I meditate every day. I try to distract myself from catastrophic thinking. I try to practise unconditional love and kindness – towards myself and others. I believe in science and yet I tap on my body's meridian points whenever I feel the trembling river of anxiety anywhere inside me. During a bad year last year – fears about my health snowballing into months of upset – the tapping was something I stumbled across. It seemed to help. And now I cling to it like a life raft. I hope it will continue to carry me clear of dangerous waters.

There are ways that panic and anxiety have made life difficult at times, stopped me from doing things I've wanted to do, enjoying things I've wanted to enjoy. Perhaps they have held me back in ways I don't know – stopping me from opening up to possibilities that might help me as a writer: being more visible, more available, more opportunistic. Perhaps they have somehow stopped me from being successful – because success would bring a whole range of new things to be afraid of: giving readings, going to literary festivals, being seen.

But perhaps there are ways that panic and anxiety have helped. Perhaps they make me the writer I am, make me more aware of my surroundings, of people's behaviour, make me more open to those small moments of joy that can burst and bloom like rainbows in a waterfall. Perhaps the mental pathways that foster creativity are the same pathways that cause anxiety – so that shutting them down would shut down the ability to write, to paint, to make. Perhaps anxiety and panic are just the dark side of having a good imagination. But who knows? I'm allowing my thoughts to gather and grow too quickly in the way they often do.

It is cold out today. There is a dusting of frost on the ground, a beautiful golden light illuminating the trees, casting long shadows beneath them. There is no movement out there – no breeze, no sign of bird in branch or sky. All is still.

But now, enough of this – enough of observing, remembering. Now I just need to get up and go outside. Into this bright December day. The sun is low but strong. It is waiting for me. And now I go.

A Disappearing Act

Kate Leaver

Kate Leaver is a journalist for Glamour, Vogue, *the* Guardian *and the* Daily Telegraph. *She is also the author of* The Friendship Cure, *in which she speaks to scientists, friends and strangers to find out why we need each other more than ever. Kate lives with her boyfriend and dog between Sydney and London.*

I was thirteen when I first wanted to disappear.

Glandular fever and then chronic fatigue syndrome had me bedridden. I missed years of school, watching *Friends* on VHS from my mother's bed, instead of learning algebra and conjugating French verbs. My parents took me to every type of medical professional we could think of, desperate to find me the energy to participate in my own youth. On this pilgrimage around the suburbs of Sydney, we visited a naturopath: could my obscene lethargy actually be a food allergy? She put me on an elimination diet – no dairy, no wheat, no yeast, no sugar, no soy – to test the possibility. Something happened as I began to forget the taste of bread and butter and chocolate: the more food groups I banished from my plate, the more powerful I felt. My waist and thighs and arms started shrinking, my school friends complimented me on my diminished figure, my sense of self blended into my feeling of hunger. A growl in my stomach felt like pride, a tremor in my hands felt like an achievement. A diabolical thought came, bidden by restriction: what if I just stopped eating altogether?

High on the feeling of getting smaller, I started to hide, throw out or regurgitate food. I turned down invitations to go out with friends, frightened by the prospect of pizza at a sleepover or ice cream at the movies. I shredded my Vegemite sandwiches into tiny pieces at lunchtime and stashed them in playground bins when my friends were distracted. I lied to my parents about when and what I ate. I dawdled at mealtimes, shifting the contents of my dinner around until I was allowed to leave the table. My days became obstacle courses: how many calories could I dodge, how many meals could I avoid, how many tastes could I refuse.

At the beginning of my disappearance, I had the perfect alibi: we had paid a woman to prescribe a restrictive diet for me in search of a diagnosis. For a time I was just following orders, existing on rice milk, pears and a ration of unsalted cashews. Then, when we called an end to my allergen search, I simply continued on my way to starvation, unaided. My life shrank as my hips did; I lived small and narrow. I didn't socialise much, I rarely made it to school, I scarcely thought about anything except food. I didn't have the energy to catch up on homework or even read; all I could do was lie in front of the television and fantasise about the texture of a snack-size Mars bar.

This continued until a tenuous school friend told her mother that she'd noticed me destroying my sandwiches. Her mother told mine, which confirmed a frightening suspicion she'd already harboured without truly understanding where a diet ends and an illness begins. I was fifteen by this time and we went on a sun-drenched, sandy-footed holiday to Queensland. I read a memoir by an Australian woman about her time with an eating disorder. She mentioned her weight loss in kilograms, wrote about her starvation techniques in prescriptive detail and inspired me to steal laxatives from the pharmacy down the road from our hotel while my mother was trying on hats. The day before we flew home, Mum found the almost-empty packet in my suitcase and confronted me. She had known for a while, without knowing she knew, that something wasn't right. I confessed, we said the word 'anorexia' out loud and booked in to see our family GP. There, I was weighed, interrogated and referred to an eating disorders specialist whose bedside manner comprised of yelling until her neck fat trembled. She recommended I stay in an eating disorders clinic at a hospital half an hour from my home in Sydney, a third-floor labyrinth of shared rooms with pallid pistachio walls and fluorescent lighting.

For five weeks I shuffled in slippered feet between my single bed and the communal room in which we whispered at our group therapy sessions. I caught the elevator down to the cafeteria (we weren't allowed to use the stairs; our predecessors had burned too many calories on those flights) three times a day to feed myself at a table of silent women, each duty-bound to finish her plate or else face the wrath of our head nurse, whose previous job was as a warden at a high-security prison. If we didn't leave our plate clean, we were sentenced to suck dry a large carton of meal replacement glug as the nurses watched.

We were only allowed home on weekends once we'd reached a certain weight. Satisfied that I was adequately expanding my waistline, the doctors approved my request to leave the hospital to rehearse for my school play, where I took on the role of Antigone's lover, clad in a spacious tunic. My then-boyfriend, a hypersensitive Rage Against the Machine fan, visited in his best leather jacket and wrote me letters. My family members sat by my bedside in turns, trying to find something to say. One praised me for my vanity – mistaking, as so many people do, an illness for a fad. This stung, because I was so sure I was motivated by something more sinister than vanity.

My anorexia was always entangled with my depression. Depression taught me to starve and starving myself fed the depression. I've been on and off antidepressants since I was twelve. As a teenager, I wanted to shrink away from the world in the only way I knew how and by denying myself food, I was essentially trying to kill myself in instalments. It was my best effort to vanish, one skipped meal at a time. It was about so much more than food, it was so much worse than a diet. It wasn't weight loss for the sake of looking good in a bikini but something darker than that, something angrier, more cruel, more hateful. When I chose not to eat, I was deliberately denying myself the nourishment to live. I was trying to make my body match the way I felt: small, weak, brittle. I became obsessed with food and the feeling its absence gave me, but it wasn't simply because I wanted to be more attractive. It was because I wanted to withdraw from the act of living my life. When you start wishing you could carve flesh off your own body just so there's less of you, you know you've gone far beyond the mentality of a diet. You forget what a normal level of vanity even means; your body doesn't feel like it belongs to you any more.

My days at the clinic were punctuated with blood tests, ECG examinations and one-on-one psychiatric sessions. I diligently attended group therapy and visited my designated medical professionals each week. I wrote letters, daydreamed about giving a speech to my peers at school about my triumphant recovery and resolutely avoided writing an essay about *Hamlet*. I gingerly made friends with young women I'd never get on with in ordinary life, clinging to them for some sort of solidarity. My doctor had warned me that sometimes patients get worse in an eating disorders clinic because anorexics like to swap starvation tips and encourage each other's disappearances. Some women get competitive with others, striving to get smaller than their companions. I never felt that. Even though I was perilously thin and depressed, I still tended to the hope that I might get better and find a way to stop caring so much about the slimness of hips. I *wanted* to get better; I just didn't quite know how.

A precious revelation came one day on a group excursion to the biggest bookshop in Sydney. Every young woman on the eating disorders ward – maybe a dozen of us – rode the escalator up in single file: a follow-the-leader of emaciated teenagers who had not been out in public for weeks. Our chaperone, a nurse, told us to look for books that would help us on our journey to recovery. Of course, several girls had to be shepherded away from the diet section and back towards something safer, like self-help or biography. Thinking of my favourite feminist teacher at school, I loitered by the gender studies books, running my fingers along spines. I picked up a copy of *Hunger Strike* by Susie Orbach. In the sequel to her seminal bestseller *Fat is a Feminist Issue*, Orbach argues that the struggles of anorexic women are a metaphor for the experience of being female in a man's world. Reading the premise of the book on its back cover, I had an inkling that it could change the way I thought about anorexia and myself. The nurse tried to steer me towards a glossy book of inspirational quotes but I clasped my Orbach stubbornly.

On my own, back in hospital, I delighted in Orbach's suggestion that eating disorders might be a symptom of patriarchy. I read about how we teach girls to diminish themselves and how we treat women's bodies as though they're public property. I started to think that maybe these deeply private afflictions – our eating disorders – were also public struggles. That there's a reason most anorexia victims are women. That my illness may not, in fact, be entirely my own fault. Orbach allowed me to shift some of the blame for my attempted disappearance outside of myself and in so doing, find some forgiveness.

Orbach's anger was contagious. She made me feel brave and strong, and angry too. I just had to find a way to turn that anger against the anorexia. In group therapy, we were asked to write a love letter to our eating disorder. That was easy enough to do because when you're anorexic, your illness becomes your closest companion. I wrote about the feelings of power and control and superiority and adrenalin it gave me. I thanked it for the pleasure of being small. Then we were asked to write a letter of hatred to our eating disorder – and that's when I really found my rage. In tiny cursive handwriting on cream paper, I seethed at what anorexia had stolen from me. I wrote about the time, the love, the friendship, the confidence and the adolescence it had taken. Personifying my illness forced me to see it as something separate from me, which brought a revelation: if anorexia was my nemesis rather than my friend, then recovery could be my revenge. I folded that vitriolic letter in half several times and stashed it in a tiny box, which I kept in my bedside table when I was finally allowed to go home permanently. I destroyed my love letter to anorexia and read through my tirade regularly, to steel myself against an inner monologue that continued to suggest starvation. I found a strength inside me that I hadn't known was there – and I ate. I ate. I ate. I ate.

With support from a psychiatrist, a psychologist, a GP and my mother, I returned to a healthy weight, able to nourish myself even when the temptation to vanish lingered. I read more about anorexia and the science of starvation. I learned about my cunning condition and felt bolder with that knowledge. I came to understand that my illness was a dangerous, chaotic mix of genetics, biology, psychology, inherited anxiety and social pressure. Knowing all that made me stronger. There was no one cause for it, just as there is no one solution. Reading *Hunger Strike* didn't cure me but it gave me the power and the permission to think about my disorder in a completely different way. It helped me find the energy to fight for my own life. It taught me that the desire to take up as little space as possible in this world was a gendered one. It comforted me with the notion that my illness did not solely belong to me. While having anorexia is a clinical condition that only affects a proportion of the population, the general desire to be small belongs to many women because of the way we as a society condition them to long for reduction. Reading Orbach taught me that my anorexia was part genetic, part societal. That was a liberating thought and one that's stayed with me all these years as I try to heal my relationship with myself, my body and my appetite.

I held onto that dangerous, spurious notion – that my weight in kilograms was a measurement of my worth as a human being – for a long time. I have wasted countless hours standing in front of the mirror, looking for signs of moral failure in the circumference of my belly. I have probably spent weeks of my precious time on this earth hating my body and panicking about pudding when I could have been thinking about my family, my beloved, my career, my future, my friends and the world in which I live. I have expended obscene amounts of energy fretting about my size and only recently have I truly noticed the full tragedy of this.

My boyfriend is hungry and thin, with a cyclist's body and a twenty-something person's metabolism. He eats what he likes – sometimes with abandon but mostly just for energy, enjoyment and nourishment. He cooks his own meals, bakes his own pastry, delights in pudding and then simply gets on with the business of living. He is utterly unaffected by guilt and shame when it comes to eating. He is the best example I have of someone with a functional, harmonious relationship with food. If he eats a whole packet of Jaffa Cakes in one sitting, he doesn't tell himself he deserves to starve for a week. He simply recycles the packaging and gets on to his next activity. This has made me so angry and jealous and exhausted that I've started trying to emulate his cheery aloofness to food.

We spent our most recent Christmas together inhaling mince pies like everyone else. We put out a lush spread on Christmas Day: roast turkey, pigs in blankets, roasties, all the trimmings and several options for pudding. We ate with festive abandon and afterwards, for the first time, I didn't panic. I didn't start making plans for January diets. I didn't dream up a fitness regime or a cleanse as my penance for enjoying Christmas. I didn't do any maths on calories. I didn't promise myself that, come 1 January, I would deny myself food to make up for all that I'd scoffed in the preceding weeks. I didn't scold myself and I didn't tell myself I was disgusting. I just kept feeding myself at mealtimes and otherwise getting on with my days. I started reading sensible food writers, nutritionists and dieticians on the topic of rejecting diet culture and its pervasiveness. I unfollowed all wellness and fitness bloggers on Instagram and replaced them with shih-tzus. I took my scales out of the bathroom, stashed them in a cupboard and stopped sneaking in to weigh myself. I consciously tried to live the life I wanted: the life of someone who eats because she needs to and because she wants to.

I have a more peaceful relationship with my body now. It's not perfect; nothing is. Some nights, I still lie in bed and tally up every morsel of food I've consumed that day with a feeling of guilt in my belly. Some days, I catch myself thinking cruel thoughts about my body. Sometimes I accidentally slip into shame once I've eaten and it takes me hours, sometimes days, to get free again. But mostly I just eat and live and eat and live.

I have learned to truly enjoy eating again: the warmth of a roast potato at the end of my fork, the joy of gelato with friends, the comfort of curry made by someone who loves me. My favourite gesture of love from recent years was when my boyfriend baked sixty choc-chip cookies so that he could spell out the title of my first book on the night of the book launch. Some of my loveliest, cosiest, most joyful moments of human connection and happiness have involved eating. In sadness and in joy, I have eaten. For comfort and for enjoyment, I have eaten. On lovely days and horrid days, I have eaten. I have eaten and eaten. I have eaten fat wedges of Cheddar on crackers for afternoon tea, Sunday roasts after a walk with my dog on Hampstead Heath, hot chimney cake sprinkled with cinnamon sugar on the streets of Prague, an enormous castle-shaped cake friends made for my thirtieth birthday, packets of Percy Pig on train trips across the countryside and boiled eggs with Vegemite-smeared soldiers for breakfast most mornings. I have learned – finally – almost two decades after I first wanted to disappear, how to eat properly and joyously. It is an unspeakable relief to feel this way.

I have the body, now, of someone who eats food. I take up more space than I ever have and I feel entitled to it.

I won't lie. Sometimes I get fragile and frantic about it. Sometimes I panic about my biscuit consumption or feel ashamed about my looks. Sometimes I forget that I am not the sum of my physical features. Sometimes I'm tempted to sneak a look at the scales, just so I have a tangible way of working out what I'm worth in a language I used to rely on. Sometimes I compare myself to other women or listen to a cruel, unforgiving private monologue about how I'm not as good or as slim or as beautiful as they are. Sometimes I make plans to start diets or exercise regimes to drastically alter my body. Sometimes when I travel to a new place or try a new medication or go through a bout of depression or watch a movie starring a particularly thin woman or try on a swimsuit or go days without sleeping, I lapse into my old anxieties about food. I'm not thunderously happy about the way I look and feel and exist at all times; this is not that kind of story. I do not have a flawless attitude and I am not immune to spells of fear and doubt and shame. But I have to say, I do live stretches of my life now without being obsessive and nasty and scared. I know how to enjoy food, I know how to share food with the people I adore and I know how to get through the hours after eating pudding without intolerable guilt.

I have officially rediscovered the joys of spaghetti and cheese and cider and apple crumble and bread with lashings of butter. I have taught myself to waste my time and energy better, thinking about wonderful frivolous things like *Love Island*, my dog's Instagram page and the characters in *Brooklyn Nine-Nine*, rather than the width of my thighs or the wobble of my biceps. I am angry about the way we belittle women, and I am hopeful, should I one day become a mother, that I could teach a daughter to fight against that. Most days, I am comfortable with who I have become. I measure my worth in the words I write and the friends I support and the man I love and the family I adore.

I no longer wish to disappear.

Three Wise Women

Irenosen Okojie

Irenosen Okojie is a Nigerian British author whose work combines the surreal and the mundane to create vivid narratives that play with form and language. Her debut novel Butterfly Fish *and her short story collection* Speak Gigantular *have won and been shortlisted for multiple awards. A fellow of the Royal Society of Literature, Irenosen lives in east London with her dog Gogo.*

That period I call winter, when life seemed unbearable and I found myself crying silently on peripheries slightly beyond the city, I thought about being unwittingly complicit in the disappearance of a woman I used to know. Who looked just like me. What I had left were her excavated bones, which I was forcing myself to survey in order to kick-start my own resurrection.

My mother used to tell me the story of how I'd nearly died as a baby. She would always mention this anecdote randomly, uncannily, whenever I was in good spirits as if to remind me to appreciate the chance I'd been given and to warn me of dangers lurking around corners. I'd suffered from frequent convulsions as a baby. Nobody knew what caused them but they greatly concerned my mother and occasionally terrified her. In one instance, I convulsed so badly I became unusually still, dead-eyed, quiet. My mother tried everything to revive me but nothing seemed to work. It had been an unbearably hot afternoon, she said, and in the evening, the moon appeared even more beautiful than usual, as if mocking her worry.

This was in Benin, Nigeria. We were staying in the rural parts and the nearest hospital was at least a two-hour drive away. My father was out of the country on a business trip. There was no time. Panicked, a little out of her mind, my mother took me to her mother, who tied me on her back and carried me into my uncle's car, a temperamental white Volkswagen Beetle. They drove to the local river, rushing down the long road until they got to the banks, where they waded into the water with me, and my grandmother reached under the surface and fed me something, some weed or part of a plant, which saved me. Many years later, when winter arrived and sucked me into its bleak depths, I thought about that image a lot: three generations of women in the water at night; an intervention, the moon as a witness.

Now that grandmother was gone. My mother had her own worries. The first few days of my winter, the start of a long period with no seasonal change, I became obsessed with finding out what my grandmother had fed me to revive me. I was fixated on that small detail. I sat in train carriages watching for a far-flung white calla lily to manifest from a rip in a seat; I wandered through museums hoping for African seaweed to spill out of my pockets; I loitered in the waiting room of my local GP longing to catch some wayward water creature through the rhythm in my chest, a creature my grandmother had sent to me from beyond the grave that had only moments left to breathe in the cloistered air of the surgery. But my grandmother had taken her secret with her, and having lived away in England since I was eight, I never thought to ask; the folly of youth. Not even my mother knew. This devastated me as a succession of traumas over the previous years had cast me into a broken place, a seemingly immovable purgatory.

Despite all my efforts to remain optimistic, I was sick. I felt hollowed out, as if my entrails were floating above the city, waiting for someone to hold them. I battled a terrible lethargy, couldn't sleep, my back hurt from stress and pressure. A searing pain shot through my chest whenever I stepped outside. A cycle of negative thoughts spun on a loop in my head and I couldn't take in the beauty of anything. The frenetic pace of living in London made it hard to pause, to appreciate the glorious light between women passing in animated conversations, the knowing gaze of a fox tailing me at night when I circled our area for a rush of cold air, the poetry of untied shoes in park trees.

I ran. I walked the dog every day. I attended a Buddhist meeting with a friend – an illuminating experience filled with angry, anarchic Buddhists arguing and interrogating what they deemed the failing of their religion to support the disenfranchised. It was wonderful to see, although I felt removed from it because I felt removed from everything during that time. At the height of my anxiety, when it really took hold of my body, I had to cancel the first speaking events for the publication of my debut short story collection – doubly traumatic as I'd worked hard for many years to reach that point.

In her book *Women Who Run with the Wolves*, Jungian psycho-analyst, poet and cantadora Clarissa Pinkola Estés argues that we must tap into our wildish nature when a woman experiences a 'gutting'. That we must leap into the desert or into the snow, and run hard, searching under, searching over, for a sign that she still lives. And that when women reclaim their relationship with their wildish nature, 'they are gifted with a permanent and internal watcher, a knower, a visionary, an oracle, an inspiratrice, an intuitive, a maker, a creator, an inventor, and a listener who guide, suggest, and urge vibrant life in the inner and outer worlds'. I returned to this quote many times during those difficult days. It was to me a rallying cry urging a woman to reach for her true self underneath all the pain of brokenness, to try not to escape that pain but to know it, sit with it, understand it, use it as fuel, then pass through it. I had to seek that internal watcher who would guide me. I had to call to her with a wild cry of my own, feel my warrior heart beating again, let the footprints of ancestors disintegrate in my blood. I just had to move.

Later that year, I travelled to Berlin for a week to run a workshop and speak at a salon event. I was struggling with imposter syndrome exacerbated by my high levels of anxiety. The room I rented was an efficient, kooky space overlooking the courtyard of an art-gallery compound in Kreuzberg. The front door to that side of the building was stiff and never opened properly with the first push, so you had to really lean into it. It was the same with my room door. This seemed metaphorical to me, reflective of how, as a black woman in the UK, I had to lean in to spaces and put my full body weight into opportunities in order to break them open for myself. All the doors on each floor looked exactly the same. I kept going up to the wrong floor and leaning in to the wrong door to the bewilderment of some patient tenant who'd open her door to find me fumbling with the knob on the other side.

My room was cold. The radiator didn't work properly. At intervals it made a thumping noise as if a stone was trapped inside it. The internet was dodgy. I outdid a contortionist in awkward corners to get moments of access. Anxiety crept in incrementally, then took hold. A day before my workshop, I was in full panic mode. By then my room was freezing and I paced back and forth trying not to crawl up the walls. What could I offer a group of emerging writers when I was myself falling apart? I decided to roam around the neighbourhood to soak up my anxious energy. I took a small notebook to jot down observations and distract myself as I walked up to the canal and then widened my exploration. I loved Berlin. I felt stubborn, determined for things to go well. And luckily, on that occasion they did.

The complex intermingling of pain and relief in art was something I constantly grappled with. It was unending, impossible to measure, a bit like time and space in continuum. I only knew that for as long as I could remember, I had always seen art as a transformative space, but true transformation comes with pain, with sacrifice, with the commitment to take a leap of faith when you do not know how you will land, with the kind of loneliness that over time becomes embedded into your DNA. For me, making art, writing in particular, was a long period of incubation and my books were languages waiting to be released, slowly forming and shaping as I felt my way through the dark, catching bits of splintered light. Eventually, I'd bend into handwriting on the page, giving communion to characters I could not shake off, carrying their dialogue in my brain like alien infiltrations, promising to know them, to leave markings over their web-like tapestries with curled fingers.

The writing life was harder than anyone had ever told me it would be. It was getting up at dawn to face a blank page when you were unsure of what you'd written two pages before; it was having nobody to guide you because in those early years much of it was hidden, secretive. I could not say I was an author because there was no finished product to show people, no book to proudly place in the hands of others, who eyed me with amusement. Writing meant awkward pauses in conversations with those who did not care for it nor understood the tumultuous nature of craft. It meant excruciating periods of waiting for what I deemed my inadequacies to improve. It meant retreating from friends to develop my writing, to live it, breathe it, envision it and make it indelible. It was – and is – a selfish endeavour, yet wholly necessary for me to function: a shared rhythm between brain and hand.

During those lonely days, the writing was a thing of wonder when it began to fall into place, when ideas came effortlessly, when a scene felt right or a character became so fully dimensional that it seemed like I was keeping her company. The joy of creating and moving through worlds was unlike any other pleasure I had ever known. It was addictive. It showed me the possibilities of language, of reaching beyond perceived limitations and into myself. Writing was something I grasped at when the world was spinning around me and nothing made sense. All I ever hoped to do was touch people, move them, make them re-examine trauma, empathy and pain by holding a lens to characters on the fringes. When I struggled, I wrote, so I could try to access the sea under the sea, the clear waters my grandmother had used to give me life again all those years before.

In her book *Bluets*, Maggie Nelson explores her fascination with the colour blue, how it winds its way through depression, divinity, desire. Each blue object, for her, takes on a meaning, becomes a symbol, a guide. My winter had been a kind of muted silvery hue, morphing objects in to a dull grey around me. Following Nelson's idea, I decided that each grey object could be a small revelation, a way of seeing through the fog. And so, a grey day was an indication to take time out for myself, maybe sit in a botanical garden somewhere and try to identify the flowers. A grey reflection in my mirror meant shifting the focus away from myself and treating a loved one

to a gift. When apples became grey, it was time to eat ram-
butan. I took Nelson's lines to mean watching for the signs
around me, paying attention and responding in kind so I felt
I had some agency and was not completely consumed by the
darkness swirling around me.

The crazy thing about all this is that I somehow managed
to write two books through this period of silver and grey. For
years, writing was a ritual for me, a survival mechanism that
had become ingrained into my very core. I had a complicated
relationship with it. It was a space I protected fiercely through
different career paths, tenuous relationships, family commitments. I needed to make things, to create worlds. I knew how
to do that. I don't know if the writing saved me, but it kept me
focused. I was driven. I needed something to show for this
time of wreckage, something I could weigh, measure and hold
up to the splinters of light occasionally seeping through, to
say, *Look at the silver I produced through the fog*. I needed concrete achievements beyond the nebulous black smoke that had
first dogged my heels before spiralling through my body.

The final time I saw my grandmother was several months
before she died. I was the last grandchild to see her alive. She
was moving about with a walking stick, having suffered two
strokes and changed drastically with age, but she still had that
old magic about her, that free spirit and wilful glint in her
eyes. Even then, I forgot to ask what she'd given me from the
river. I forgot to say thank you for saving my life. We broke
bread, looked at old photographs, danced and drank palm
wine together. We had the same arms, the same hands, the

same buoyant disposition at our best. I cried on the plane back to London thinking about it.

Maybe you wonder what wise women the title of this essay alludes to. Perhaps it's my grandmother, my mother and me. Or maybe it's my grandmother, Clarissa Pinkola Estés and Maggie Nelson, women from different cultures who've mined their experiences to show us the shape of light lurking beneath. Perhaps it's me as a baby, me as a young girl and me now, still finding my way. Or maybe it's three wise women inside all women, speaking to us from the bottom of a river, waiting for us with silvery gifts so we can revive ourselves when winter arrives again.

Last Fragments of Love

Cathy Rentzenbrink

Cathy Rentzenbrink is the author of The Last Act of Love *and* A Manual for Heartache. *Despite being shortlisted for various prizes, the only thing Cathy has ever won is the Snaith and District Ladies' Darts Championship when she was seventeen. She is now sadly out of practice.*

The first time was just after my twentieth birthday. I was in my first year at Leeds University, which was about twenty miles away from where my parents lived in our pub with my brother, Matty. Two and a half years earlier, Matty had been knocked over by a car and nearly died. He was left in a persistent vegetative state and we had built an extension to care for him at home. There was no evidence at all of any possible recovery but, against all logic, we continued to hope that one day he might suddenly smile or speak or tell us a joke. I hadn't wanted to leave him behind and go away to university but my parents thought I should. I chose the closest possible place and went home every weekend.

So, Leeds, 1993. The winter was harsh and the cold bit at my cheeks and fingers as I shuffled between my room in Lupton flats and the campus. On Valentine's Day I finished with my boyfriend. That wasn't very nice, but I wasn't fitted for any sort of adult relationship. The thing I wanted from any man was to be my brother, so having sex felt incestuous and wrong. I didn't explain that to anyone, of course. I went home a bit less often after that. All our customers at the pub thought I'd dumped my boyfriend because I was getting posh and stuck up, and it was bizarre to be treated like a femme fatale when I felt so broken. Also, I was finding it harder to drive my car. I'd never been a good driver and I didn't pass my test until the fourth time, but I seemed to be getting worse rather than better. I'd get in a muddle and panic. And, of course, although I didn't admit it to myself, perhaps I was beginning to question how much point there was in continuing to talk to Matty as though he still existed. How much longer could I bear to gaze into his open eyes looking in vain for any vestige of his old intelligence and charm? Where had he gone? Would he come back? And, if he didn't, how would I live?

In Leeds I adored my neighbour, Sophie, who was the first person I met when I arrived. We'd stay up late drinking red wine and playing Scrabble and then I'd go to bed and cry. I missed Matty. I kept pining for another world where the accident hadn't happened and he would come to visit us. I could picture him cramming his enormously long legs under our kitchen table and making everyone laugh. I'd be amusing, too, in that other world. More jokes and less crying and brooding.

I was increasingly unable to go to my tutorials because I'd forgotten how to speak French. I'd been so good at it but now the words swirled. I felt inferior to my fluent classmates, who seemed to have grown up spending summers with French relatives. I had grown up teased for being clever and posh; I didn't have much of a Yorkshire accent due to my Irish father and Cornish mother. It was a shock to find out that I certainly wasn't posh and I didn't seem to be clever any more, either. My much-celebrated gift of the gab – my dad liked to say that I'd had no need to kiss the Blarney Stone – had vanished. I had nothing to say to anyone in any language.

I didn't want to leave the flat. I remember standing in the nearby supermarket in Headingley, staring into other people's baskets to try to piece together some clue as to what I should buy. Everything was absurd. All my clothes were dirty but I was scared of the laundry room. The business of trying to work out how to operate the machines, what combination of change was needed and how to buy soap powder was beyond me. I'd lie in bed for hours, listening to my thudding heart, smoking and pondering my laundry crisis but unable to summon up the energy to do anything about it.

I'm hazy about how it came around, but eventually my mother picked me up and drove me to a retreat in north Leeds. I'd been to a Catholic school and was used to the notion of going on retreat, so the place felt familiar: a rather run-down, not-quite-stately home up a tree-lined drive. There were daffodils everywhere. My mum checked me in and found out about meals for me so I wouldn't have to say anything. My room was simple: a single bed, a desk, a crucifix on the wall by the window. We sat on the bed and she cuddled me. She said if I didn't like it, I could ring her up and she'd come and get me. She said, 'Perhaps I could have another child. Would that make things any better for you?'

I sobbed and sobbed. I was overwhelmed by her kindness but I didn't want a new sibling, a baby, I wanted my own brother back to how he was. I wanted what had happened not to have happened.

Retreat life was OK. There were religious types knocking around if you wanted to talk to them, but I didn't. I went to Mass. I liked the monastic vibe of my little room and I spent most of my time there, reading books from the huge library. I felt a million years old. During meals, I looked at the other people – all at least a generation older than me – and wondered what had brought them to this place. I could never have guessed, I thought, when I was at school, that by the age of twenty I'd be the sort of grown-up who came somewhere like this on her own.

Mum picked me up after a few days and drove me back to my flat. She'd tidied up, changed the bed and washed all my clothes. She told me she'd arranged for me to see a therapist on Tuesday nights and that she and Dad were going to come and take me out for lunch on Thursdays. She'd talked to the university and I wasn't in any trouble for missing lectures.

The therapist was called Jane. I always felt nervous about going, mainly because I had to drive there in the dark and would often get lost or struggle to park. Once that bit was over, I'd find myself relaxing as I walked up her drive. She saw me in the front room of her house. There was a Klimt print on the wall, a couch and a green beanbag. I only ever sat in an armchair but I enjoyed flirting with the notion that one day I might choose a different seat. There were boxes of tissues dotted around the place and the first thing I'd do would be to suss out where the nearest box was and then play a game with myself about how long I could last without reaching for it.

I told Jane all about Matty's accident and its aftermath. It was here I began to admit that I could see Matty wasn't going to get better, that there would be no magical awakening, that love and effort and hoping would not be able to reverse his brain damage. Jane diagnosed me with post-traumatic stress disorder. The weeks went by. She helped me be less angry and insular and I learned to keep my misery for her. Whenever something distressed me between sessions, I would make a mental note to discuss it with Jane and that would help me hold myself together. I no longer cried indiscriminately but managed, largely, to keep my tears for Jane's tissue box. I could lead something like a normal life, I realised, I could have friends, if I mastered this magic trick of boxing all my anguish away into one secret place.

Fast forward twenty-two years and my book about Matty, *The Last Act of Love*, had just come out. It had taken me years to write and I hadn't imagined that anyone would want to read it, but I was overwhelmed by the kindness and connection that followed. I raced around the country doing events and interviews. When people asked me how I had written the book, I could hardly remember. Often, if I didn't have it in my hand, I might think that I had made it up. Not the story itself – for ever inked on my heart – but the writing of it, the publishing of it, the fact that people cared.

'What does it feel like to be a bestselling author?' people would ask me.

I'd smile and not know who they were talking about.

I had my photo taken several times. All these different versions of myself kept looking back at me, daring me to try and work out which one was real. None of them looked like the woman with the grey hungover face who stared back from my bathroom mirror every morning.

When I was little, we had a dressing table with a mirror in three pieces. The central bit was static but the two side panels moved. I'd sit in the middle and move the mirrors and see multiple selves reflected back at me. I'd do this for ages, fascinated by the way I looked from different angles. I felt now like all these different angles, all these different representations were out in the world and I didn't know how to keep a grip on them.

In the middle of August, my husband Erwyn and I went to stay with Sophie and assorted other friends and relatives of hers in a large house in the Dordogne for a few days. Sophie picked us up from Limoges airport in her Volkswagen camper van. She looked so beautiful and I felt full of joy and gratitude that she was my friend and had been for so many years. This was the life, I thought; I'd weathered storms galore, but now was a time of ease and pleasure.

We'd left our son, Matt, in Cornwall with my parents, which had seemed like a good idea for all sorts of logistical reasons, but I missed him with a horrible intensity, as though my maternal panic button had been activated. The metaphorical umbilical cord wouldn't stop twitching.

The farmhouse was big and dark. Outside was full of flying things and wasp traps. A lizard raced over my flip-flopped toes. I can cope with creatures when I am well, can even do bug handling with Matt at wildlife centres, but it's one of the first accomplishments to desert me when I start to slide, together with driving or even being in a car. That afternoon we headed to the supermarket along the winding lanes and I could feel roiling anxiety whipping itself up inside me. I've never been good at being on holiday. I'm at my best with plenty to do and preferably some juicy problems to solve. I'm skilled at finding silver linings, far less adept at coping when there are no clouds.

Every night, as it grew dark, we sat outside, drank negronis and played the werewolf game. This involved having to work out which of us were the innocent villagers and which were the werewolves that would destroy the village. It called for lots of duplicity, betrayals and recriminations. I kept thinking how, if you felt like an outsider in a family group, playing this game would create a tinderbox situation, and I began to work on a story that was exactly that – sinister undertones during a family holiday where the rough-trade boyfriend of one of the posh sisters felt increasingly left out and angry.

And then the rain. After three days of sunshine, the fourth brought apocalyptic levels of rain. I sat at the table, vilely hung-over, trying to write my werewolf story but feeling panic overtake me as I looked out at the water lashing down and thought of how often rain was a companion to me going mad. Leeds, Holland, France, London. I remembered my first proper bout after Matt was born. I was so relieved to have dodged the bullet of postnatal depression that I felt like the victory would endure. That turned out not to be true and I was devastated. How could I be so miserable when I had so much? I longed to be fixed, not for myself, but for Matt. I didn't want him to grow up with a mad mother.

I spent the whole day watching my every breath in and out so I wouldn't hyperventilate. The only thing to do was get drunk again, which would obliterate the fear. By night, I was carefree again, brave and drunk enough to swim in the lake before sliding into a few hours of restless intoxicated sleep. The next morning I'd wake in panic and breathe my way through a few hours of torment before drinking again. I carried on that pattern for the rest of the holiday. I gave up on writing, but reading was, as ever, an ally in taking my mind away from itself. I'd enjoyed playing word games at the start of the holiday but couldn't do it by the end. The letters wouldn't behave. I could still manage the werewolf game, though, as it fitted with my levels of paranoia and panic.

By the time we got to the airport to go home, my hands were shaking and I felt like I was disintegrating. It was a smallish plane and we boarded by climbing up a metal stairway which they'd wheeled out across the runway. Halfway up, I looked down at my feet to see the ground below and thought I might slide through the rungs. There were people in front of me and behind. I couldn't move anywhere. I clutched on to Erwyn and shut my eyes. I thought if I looked down again I might die.

I just about held it together on the flight but the drive home from Stansted was excruciating. I tensed up in the seat, so frightened of the other cars I kept flinching and twitching, my foot pounding an imaginary brake.

Back at home, I went straight to bed and lay there shivering, my heart thudding. I hadn't felt this crazy for years. I had a couple of days to gather myself together before getting the sleeper train down to Cornwall to be reunited with Matt. The main thing was to have a couple of days off drinking. I knew it wasn't rocket science. I knew it was asking for trouble to drink so much for so many days in a row after a period of extreme mental excitement. It was all about the booze, I decided.

A month later, I did an event in a church and was interviewed by the vicar, a kindly, intelligent man who asked good questions. He wanted to read out the part in my book where I talk about learning that damage could be cherished rather than denied:

> I know I'm damaged. As I've walked through fire, bits of me have burnt off – but I accept that. I've come across a new word. Kintsugi is a Japanese style of ceramics where broken

crockery is mended in an intentionally obvious way. Rather than try to hide the crack, it is filled in with gold and the breakage becomes a part of the object's story. I love this idea. I think how I am often drawn to broken people and find them beautiful. I have decided that I can stop yearning to be fixed or trying to hide the scars: I can decide to think of my broken-ness as an integral and even beautiful part of me. I've gathered up all my scattered selves and don't feel fragmented any more.

I enjoyed the vicar's voice, sonorous, used to the acoustics in his house of God, but I couldn't recognise the passage. He said it showed an astonishing level of acceptance and I agreed, except I couldn't remember thinking it or feeling it or writing it. I didn't remember being wise enough to have thought that. I felt completely disconnected from that person. Where had she gone?

Later, I realised I had done again what I'd pledged not to do. I felt so good when I finished the book – such a sense of pride to have wrestled the story onto the page – that I allowed myself to feel fixed. Now I was disintegrating once more and didn't know what to do. My selves had scattered again. I was fragmenting all over the place. And I felt like a fraud.

Another three years have passed. More therapy, more reading and writing, more tangling with myself, often feeling that the more I learn about depression, the less I know. I stopped drinking alcohol eighteen months ago, which has hugely reduced my anxiety and helped me do the things I know I need to do to stay in a good place. I am not depressed at the moment. My mood is fairly stable. I laugh and cry a lot. I used to fear my tears, and worry that crying would lead to not being able to stop, but I have learned that feeling sad is not sinister and it is better to allow tears to fall rather than choke them off. It is not socially acceptable, of course. We are supposed to grow out of it. The only reason I stop myself is because I don't want to embarrass or distress anyone. But if I know and trust my company, I allow myself to be a watering can. I compare it to bleeding the radiator.

When I think back to those days in Leeds, I can see that I didn't want to accept that my brother would be better off dead. I'm no longer surprised that, finding life so unpalatable, I couldn't get out of bed. Nor does it seem especially strange that in the early days of my story being out in the world, I struggled to hold myself together. I'd blown my own cover and invited other people to see the contents of my box of despair; I needed a bit of time to adjust. Looking back down the years of my life, it's clear to me that my depressive episodes, though they seemed irrational at the time, all had something to do with refusing to accept an unpleasant reality or being frightened that if the world knew what I was really like, it would find me inadequate.

Not being depressed is a cause for celebration, of course, though I am cautious. Am I free or only out on parole? Over the twenty-five years of being locked in what can feel like mortal combat – but what I try to think of as a dance – I've learned not to get too smart. If I don't want to go back to prison, I have to make sure I keep the conditions of my bail. They are not too onerous. No booze, be careful with technology and social media and news consumption, eat well, take exercise, get plenty of fresh air, don't allow myself to get too cold and hungry. Be curious, compassionate, gentle, creative. Accept that sometimes I will be sad, angry and frightened. Work out how to let my emotions breathe rather than bottle them up. I feel a bit of a princess, sometimes, with all this quackery, but I know that if I don't look after myself, I will end up not like the princess but like the pea, flattened and suffocating under the weight of the world.

A therapist friend of mine suggested that I stop using the word depression and try to think of my moods more like the weather. There will be different days, but I can console myself that I have all kinds of wellies, umbrellas and waterproofs. And the sun will come out again. Right now, there is an actual, rather than metaphorical, gale blowing outside my window. I'm not frightened of the rain any more. When it clears, I will walk down to the cemetery and find the plaque on my granny's grave in memory of my brother. I'll sit on the side of the grave. I might well cry. I might say, 'Why the fuck are you not here?' I might tell him a couple of jokes. I'll be myself, and that includes still missing him, still longing for him, still feeling staggered by the sheer awful sadness of everything that happened. But I have – finally, just about – been able to accept that my real last act of love for Matty is to look after myself, and his nephew and namesake, and to try to live well in a world without him.

Not Wasted

Ed Mitchell

For many years, Ed was a successful broadcast journalist at organisations such as BBC, Reuters, ITN and CNBC. After a troubled relationship with alcohol, he ended up sleeping rough on the streets. With luck and a desire to live, he learned from the experience and wrote about it. Ed now lives by the English Channel and swims there most mornings.

I've been wrestling with alcohol for over half a century. Sometimes I'm on top, other times I'm flat on my back, firmly in its grip. Exhausting though the struggle is, I keep getting back in the ring.

It didn't start as a fight. Quite the opposite – it was love at first taste. My relationship with alcohol began as a passionate affair in the optimistic sunshine of youth. That first sip of cider at the age of sixteen has a treasured place in my memory. It felt instantly right, filling my brain and limbs with warmth, excitement and euphoria. Everything seemed possible.

It was a first drink conducted almost like an experiment in

my parents' back garden in 1969. The sun beamed out of a clear blue sky, butterflies filled nearby shrubs, the flowers hummed with bees and in the background, birdsong: a moment preserved in time. It's a scene and a feeling I've been trying to recapture ever since. The passage of decades has made this a frustrating pursuit.

Alcohol gave me something that was missing. It's hard to define what this missing 'something' actually was, but alcohol seemed to fill the gap. I became confident, comfortable in my skin and at ease with other people. For an introverted teenager, this was miraculous. It seemed to me at the time that all the 'good guys' drank and being one of them was important to that teenage me.

Good times became so closely tied to drinking that fun times could not actually be had without it. This drink/fun connection translated seamlessly to life at university (Durham) but it had other advantages, too. Homesickness, a sense of state-school inferiority and the need to fit in could all be alleviated (or blotted out) by consuming gallons of beer. I was good at it.

Joining rugby and rowing clubs, writing for the university newspaper and becoming college president provided ample opportunities and excuses to drink, though they were also enjoyable in themselves. It felt natural to consume beer, not a hint of it being a problem. And why would it be? Hangovers were easily handled and all the in-crowd drank. Good blokes played hard, worked hard, got the good degrees – and the girls. Those were the best days of my life.

The good times continued to roll, albeit in a different way. From Durham it was straight into Fleet Street as a graduate trainee with Reuters. Having a close relationship with alcohol fitted in perfectly with the atmosphere and ethos of the Street, which in the 1970s was still home to all the main newspapers. The area was filled with the smells of paper, printer's ink and a beery aroma wafting from the doors of countless pubs. What drove the Street was the mantra: 'Get the story, get it first, get it right, get the drinks in.' To me, an enthusiastic, impressionable twenty-two-year-old, the best journalists displayed a worldly, hardbitten attitude, met their contacts in bars and operated well while intoxicated.

My first foreign posting was to Hong Kong. At that time, more than twenty years before the handover of the colony to China, the place still retained much of its colonial atmosphere: European-only clubs, non-Chinese living areas, big swash-buckling trading companies and a hard-working/hard-playing lifestyle that involved hefty, stiff gin and tonics. The quinine-containing tonic was, of course, just to ward off malaria.

Back from Hong Kong, I moved over to the BBC for the next ten years, broadcasting on radio and television. Speaking live into a microphone or facing a camera never felt entirely comfortable until I'd had a few drinks to settle things down. Getting just the right balance between cool confidence and slurring gibberish was always the key issue. Occasionally – but increasingly frequently – I was getting that important calcula-tion wrong and it was beginning to be noticed.

By this stage, I had a wife, two children, a large mortgage and was commuting by train from the south coast to London five days a week: the usual lot of a working person. People have their own ways of handling these demands; in my case, it was self-medicating through alcohol. It took the harsh edge off daily survival and helped me function.

Drinking had now evolved from good fun to something darker. I was using it to control my mood, topping up every day and feeling bleak and down if I didn't. Life without alcohol was grey and flat. I was chasing after the sunshine of my youth, but I had to drink more and more to return to that happy place.

I didn't think I had a problem, but I got a harsh reality check at the end of 1999 when I was sacked from my £90,000-a-year job at CNBC for an alcohol-related incident. The reason I mention my salary is because it had sustained a high level of easily available credit. That debt mountain was now unsustainable on zero income and the house of plastic cards came tumbling down. I desperately floundered around for the next six years, taking on any sort of job, at any pay, trying to keep the family ship sailing. It meant building up more debt, paying one credit card with another (I had twenty-five) and using loans to cover the mortgage. My income barely paid the interest due on only one of the cards.

Throughout this time I was keeping our perilous finances and my alcohol dependency a secret – or thought I was. Secrecy and self-delusion go hand in hand with alcoholism.

Alcoholics will go to elaborate lengths to hide their levels of consumption – something the industry makes easier with products like vodka miniatures or those cleverly shaped quarter bottles ideal for pockets, briefcases and handbags. They even sell picnic 'mixers' – ready-made gin and tonics with wide-necked bottles for that quick furtive slurp in the street or the toilet. Mints, chewing gum and mouthwash are also part of the cover (although some mouthwashes are 25 per cent alcohol and tempting to swallow during extreme need!).

Alcohol dependency was taking a toll on my marriage. We'd been together for twenty-five years and my wife had witnessed how drinking had gradually got a terrible hold on me. She had tried to intervene, but all attempts had failed. In lucid moments, I revealed the calamitous state of our finances, which had been hidden for years. Bankruptcy was the only way out. These were agonising times: divorce came first, then the family house was sold and the much-expanded mortgage paid off. The equity was split and I used my share to keep the credit cards alive for a few more months.

In the end, by mid-2006, I found myself with absolutely nothing: no family, no house, nowhere to live, no possessions, no car (no licence), no income, no access to credit and no idea of what would happen next. I had blotted out any thought of the future. Initially, this did not trouble me too much – bit of a challenge, a fresh start, I thought. Still, I had to sleep some-where. After a period of short-term sofa-surfing, brief stays at council shelters and a difficult three-week residency at the local Emmaus Community, I was left with one option – rough sleeping on the streets.

Following several painful early mistakes, I found what seemed like a safe park bench behind a nightclub on Hove seafront. There were half a dozen of us street sleepers (quite a few ex-soldiers), so that gave some feeling of security, even camaraderie. A public toilet was also handily close. It's important to be seen by the rough-sleepers' team, although you only become 'official' if you've been found horizontal and unconscious. And becoming 'official' means the process of getting help can begin – such as it was.

The long, mostly sleepless nights on that bench provided plenty of time to reflect on my rapid fall from successful broadcaster and family man who had travelled the world and interviewed presidents, prime ministers, chancellors and CEOs to a street tramp whose entire possessions were contained in a rucksack. There was no one to blame, nor did I want to. I could see how I was responsible, however tempting it was to slip into victimhood.

Rough sleeping is quite simply awful, painful and exhausting. It's also virtually impossible to get out of. To the local authority, a male between eighteen and sixty-five (I was fifty-four) who is not mentally or physically disabled is 'non-priority'. I made every effort to speak to various local agencies, but they were inundated with help-seekers and there was little coordination between offices. Not having an address (often associated with being homeless!) presented yet another problem: a catch-22.

Homelessness was also profoundly embarrassing. I did everything I could to stay clean and not sink into the stereotypical image of a dosser. I was a white-collar tramp. Trying to exist below the radar, in anonymity, I disappeared for a year: a seafront ghost. It was an existence that involved some tough physical challenges and harsh exposure to the elements. The cold was bad but the rain was worse. I remember one particular night when a long slog into driving rain by Hove seafront finally ended at 'my' bench. Soaked through, I resorted to my liquid comfort, a quarter bottle of vodka. Disastrously, it slipped through my cold, wet fingers and smashed on the concrete pavement – bad enough but made worse when I tried to clear the broken glass and found it immersed in dog's excrement. At least I think it was a dog's.

The only people who knew of my existence were charity workers visiting at night with coffee, sandwiches and the Word of the Lord. I was just glad of their kindness, the food and the company. Many days would pass without speaking to anyone. One of my nocturnal visitors happened to be a local journalist who recognised me from my broadcasting days. It was just ten days to Christmas and he thought my plight would make a good story – riches-to-rags, no room at the inn, homeless at Yuletide. My view was that I had nothing left to lose.

The next day, oiled by a few free beers, I was interviewed and photographed. I thought it'd make a few column inches in the Brighton *Argus*. Instead it turned out to be a front-page splash headlined 'Lost It All' and a double-page spread inside. Outside, shop billboards around town proclaimed, 'TV star loses everything' (star?). The story swiftly spread to the national newspapers, radio and television, and even internationally (it was apparently big in India and Switzerland). From lonely anonymity, I was suddenly plunged into the full glare of the public eye, at one point holding an impromptu 'press conference' – in a pub, naturally. All this attention made me feel ambivalent. The public exposure of my destitution was uncomfortable, but I had run out of options to extricate myself from the hole I was in. As an added bonus, wads of cash were being thrust into my hand by various media people; I used it to upgrade from cheap white cider to something smoother and stronger.

A documentary maker contacted me. The idea was to make a quick film in the few days remaining before Christmas, with ITN presenter Carol Barnes as the reporter who would 'discover' me on the park bench. (Carol died a few months later.) Now, a film about a homeless alcoholic needs good pictures of intoxication and raw emotion; more cash, swiftly spent on drink, made that possible. Tears do make better TV, but mine flowed naturally through exhaustion and remorse.

The half-hour documentary *Saving Ed Mitchell* (the title made me cringe) was squeezed between two episodes of *Coronation Street* and was viewed by over 5 million people. It's on YouTube and still very painful for me to watch. The media attention also resulted in a book deal and a ten-week deadline to write it – an interesting exercise if you haven't touched a keyboard for over a year. The book, *From Headlines to Hard Times*, sold reasonably well, helped by the documentary and a serialisation in the *Mail on Sunday*.

Perhaps the greatest outcome of my escape was the chance to go on a twenty-eight-day rehabilitation programme at the Priory Hospital in Roehampton, thanks to someone who worked with the clinic. It's an upmarket sort of place set in its own leafy grounds and attended by many high-profile (so-called) celebrities. The price tag for a month's stay is five figures. For my part, I was exhausted, had lost a lot of weight and was simply glad of a comfortable bed, three good meals and the opportunity to tackle my alcohol dependence.

It was a while, in the endless hours of group therapy, before I could bring myself to actually say out loud that I was an alcoholic. Apart from it being true, this admission seemed to be the only way to make progress in a regime based on the Twelve Steps of Alcoholics Anonymous. Step One of AA is to admit that you are powerless over alcohol and that your life has become unmanageable as a result. Well, I seemed to tick those boxes. Daily attendance at AA meetings in the area, reached by minibus, was obligatory, so I simply relaxed into the fellowship of the gatherings. But I never thought that advancing through the Steps or getting a 'sponsor' was ever going to be for me. I did, however, understand and appreciate the underlying philosophical roots of AA and that it has worked for thousands over the last eight decades.

Abstinence lasted for a couple of years. I felt better, though not dramatically so. Thoughts crept into my head that I could probably handle a drink, maybe two. The first mouthful was like getting in touch with an old friend and being instantly (if only briefly) transported to a version of that youthful feeling of sunshine and euphoria. But this state of mind needed topping up with further doses; as they say in AA (they are fond of aphorisms), 'One is too many and a thousand is never enough.'

I was back in that firm, craving grip, a rapid return to round-the-clock drinking. Then my mother died, which impacted me in ways I was not fully aware of at the time – or even am today. I was also working on three demanding month-long contracts training TV presenters for new broadcast companies in Bangladesh, Delhi and Nigeria. (Some of my old skills had not been entirely erased.) The result was an alcohol crisis and a return to rehab, this time at the Providence Projects in Boscombe, near Bournemouth. The therapy regime there was a lot tougher than at the Priory – more like a boot camp.

Once again, the foundations were group therapy, writing, housework and daily AA meetings around town. Accommodation was in ordinary houses near the rehab centre in groups of half a dozen men or women. The idea was to generate responsibility, self-reliance and camaraderie. Certainly, a platoon-like ethos developed over the four weeks. Weekly prizes were given for the cleanest and best-run houses.

It was hard and many fell by the wayside – Boscombe is full of off-licences and pubs. I stuck the course but the statistics for Twelve Step-based rehabs are not encouraging. There's a heavy reliance on getting a group of sick people to sit together over many hours and feel emotions in the hope that it produces long-term wellness, but two out of three fail to sustain abstinence. I managed to stay on the rails for a year or so, but then the old brain patterns re-emerged.

Over the last ten years since my escape from the park bench, the main driving force has been simply to keep going. Life is worth living – on balance. I do actually want to see what happens next. And this is a point I want to emphasise: I am alive because I just have to keep putting one foot in front of the other. I *must* cling on.

It also helps to have someone close and important in my life. I got to know Mandy in the darkest days of rough sleeping, when she brought me coffee and soup. An enthusiastic drinker herself at that time, she gave up quickly and completely when I went into the Priory. We married a few years later.

Without alcohol running through my system – when it hasn't got its hooks in me – drinking actually has little attraction. I can walk through the stacked alcohol aisles of local supermarkets without the urge to fill my trolley. Indeed, our flat is above a convenience shop with an off-licence and our road has six outlets for alcohol, but I don't use them. Booze is everywhere and I accept its existence; it's never going away.

The trouble comes, for reasons I can never understand, when the 'other' me begins to argue it's safe to revisit my old friend. Its case goes something like this: 'Look how well you feel. You could feel even better with just one drink. It'll be like the old times when you were young and life was filled with opportunity and excitement. Go on! What harm will one drink do? Don't be a bore!'

But – the thought process goes – if one drink makes you feel better (which it does), then many more will make you feel very much better. It's at this point that stopping is not possible because coming back down is too horrific. The next stage is the torture of the early-morning hours, when the only 'cure' seems to be to gulp more of the stuff that caused the problem in the first place.

This madness will be hard for non-alcoholics to understand: 'Why not just stop? Snap out of it! Get a grip!' But it's just not that simple. The compulsion to drink comes in very subtle, beguiling, convincing and crafty forms. Even though I am familiar with these voices, even though I know their siren song, I can still become wrecked on the rocks. Yes, it's 'all in the mind', but where else would it be? The question is where do these thoughts and urges come from?

In the beginning, of course, decades ago, it felt like a choice; there appeared to be the possibility of exercising free will. Over the years, the power of free will, or what feels like free will, diminishes. The habit of drinking, in association with the perception of good times, slowly carves deep neural pathways – ruts that become hard to escape.

For most people, alcohol is not a problem. They can stop at one drink, recork an unfinished bottle of wine and happily take months off. Then there's a minority prone not only to take enthusiastically to alcohol but to become dependent on it. A proportion of those will die as a result. It's not just a gene or even an array of genes; it's an interaction of many genes that express themselves in response to environmental influences, including the nutrition, famines, hardship and pollution encountered by the previous generation.

Intriguingly, in my case – and everyone is unique – the compulsion to consume alcohol can simply fade for no apparent reason. The inner voices urging me to drink are stilled. Serenity reigns and I am comfortable in my own skin. Blessed are these moments. I have tried to pin down what causes this. Is it hormonal changes? Is it something to do with nutrition? Sleep patterns? Phases of the moon? Solar activity? Whatever it is, I am grateful – until the next storm front arrives. That's when I have learned to batten down the hatches, hide myself away, let the alcohol get me through without too much damage and get off it again as soon as possible.

More recently, I returned to full-time broadcasting at a new nationwide business radio station called Share Radio. My role was to present a live four-hour show in the middle of the day with at least twelve interviews per show. It was good to be back in a studio but also draining, since the small team putting the programme together was young and inexperienced – seat-of-the pants broadcasting. The audience was small and the feedback almost non-existent.

After two years of this, I began to feel the return of the alcohol siren call: a vodka miniature before broadcasting, an immediate need for a stiff drink coming off air and increased beers on the train home. Coupled with this, the radio station was downsizing due to lack of advertising revenue. It was clearly time to part company, as I could see health problems brewing. Subsequently, Share Radio ceased broadcasting. I have worked for so many television and radio stations over the years that have gone under. No causal link, I hope.

What has kept me going for more than fifty years of drinking is, at least in the later decades, awareness of the problem, a desire to live, sheer brute stubbornness, a great deal of reading on the subject (books have constantly saved the day) and a focus on developing a personal philosophy. That philosophy, a work in progress, is a patchwork of threads selected from a sewing box of ideas, mostly ancient. It's an enduring attempt to create personal meaning. At the heart of it lies Stoicism, which is about much more than dour resilience. In many ways, it can be summed up in the Serenity Prayer that we all had to learn in rehab and recite together at the end of group therapy and AA meetings:

> Grant us the serenity to accept the things we cannot change; the courage to change the things we can and the wisdom to know the difference.

In other words, the only aspect of life you can really control is your reaction to events and people.

Looking back, almost all the mistakes I have made in my life come down to excessive consumption of alcohol. I occasionally speculate and ruminate on how different things might have been without booze. It's futile and pointless, of course; what matters is that I simply got through it all (so far). The most fortunate escape was getting out of permanent homelessness. Only my past as someone recognisable from television got me out of that deep ditch. Most of those I slept alongside a decade ago are dead. Good luck rescued me – but responding to that luck played its part too.

We all create stories, constantly but mostly unknowingly, about ourselves, tweaking and adapting them as we move through life. This is the foundation of sustaining a coherent self. It's about giving ourselves a reference point, relevance and purpose. It's the only way we function in life. This search for meaning and some sort of workable answers to the mystery of existence is, for me, a key part of 'keeping going'. Not being pissed all the time makes this quest that much easier.

I began by using wrestling as a metaphor for my long relationship with alcohol. But have I been wrestling? Perhaps I've been gripping life, clinging to it, hugging it closer, fearing its loss as it slips through my fingers. I want things to slow right down. I've no willpower to wrestle any more. I tell myself that it's only a fight if I choose to perceive it as a fight. But over the decades that perception has shifted, the battle evolved into acceptance and, with it, the realisation that I am not my opponent and that life – what remains of it – is there to be embraced.

II. Self

Self-Knowledge

David Whyte

Self-knowledge is not fully possible for human beings. We do not reside in a body, a mind or a world where it is achievable or from the point of being interesting, even desirable. Half of what lies in the heart and mind is potentiality; resides in the darkness of the unspoken and unarticulated and has not yet come into being: this hidden unspoken half of a person will supplant and subvert any present understandings we have about ourselves.

Human beings are always, and always will be, a frontier between what is known and what is not known. The act of turning any part of the unknown into the known is simply an invitation for an equal measure of the unknown to flow in and re-establish that frontier: to reassert the far horizon of an individual life; to make us what we are – that is, a moving edge between what we know about ourselves and what we are about to become. What we are actually about to become or are afraid of becoming always trumps and rules over what we think we are already.

The hope that a human being can achieve complete honesty and self-knowledge with regard to themselves is a fiction and a chimera, the jargon and goals of a corporate educational system brought to bear on the depths of an identity where the writ of organising language does not run. Self-knowledge includes the understanding that the self we want to know is about to disappear. What we can understand is the way we occupy this frontier between the known and the unknown, the way we hold the conversation of life, the figure we cut at that edge, but a detailed audit of the self is not possible and diminishes us in the attempt to establish it; we are made on a grander scale, half afraid of ourselves, half in love with immensities beyond any name we can give.

Self-knowledge is often confused with transparency, but knowledge of the self always becomes the understanding of the self as a confluence; a flowing meeting of elements, including all the other innumerable selves in the world, not a set commodity to be unearthed and knocked into shape. Self-knowledge is not clarity or transparency or knowing how everything works, self-knowledge is a fiercely attentive form of humility and thankfulness, a sense of the privilege of a particular form of participation, coming to know the way we hold the conversation of life and perhaps, above all, the miracle that there is a particular something rather than an abstracted nothing and we are a very particular part of that particular something.

What we recognise and applaud as honesty and transparency in an individual is actually the humble demeanour of the apprentice, someone paying extreme attention, to themselves, to others, to life, to the next step, which they may survive or they may not; someone who does not have all the answers but who is attempting to learn what they can about themselves and those with whom they share the journey, someone like everyone else, wondering what they and their society are about to turn into. We are neither what we think we are nor entirely what we are about to become, we are neither purely individual nor fully a creature of our community, but an act of becoming that can never be held in place by a false form of nomenclature. No matter our need to find a place to stand amidst the onward flow of the world, the real foundation of the self is not in self-knowledge but in the self-forgetfulness that occurs when it meets something other than the self it wanted to know.

My Unremembered Life

Emily Reynolds

Emily Reynolds writes for the Guardian, Observer, Vogue, NY Magazine, Times Literary Supplement *and others. Her first book,* A Beginner's Guide to Losing Your Mind, *came out in 2017; she is currently working on her second, an exploration of technology's mediation of intimacy. She lives in London.*

Memory is what makes us human: who are we without it? Our joys and miseries, our heartbreaks and intimacies and fears, the people we carry with us, who live inside us. We're all so frightened of losing our memories, by ageing or by accident, because to lose your memory is to lose your identity, your sense of self. It's to lose the most fundamental part of who you are. I remember almost nothing.

My only memories, really, come from stories. The time I stood stock-still in the middle of the living room, aged five, so utterly terrified by the electrician who had come to fix the wiring that I was paralysed, unable to move at all: that memory comes from my mother. The times, as a teenager, when I behaved irrationally about boys, broke rules, cried, laughed, had my first cigarette, got drunk, flashed on webcam, answered back to teachers: my best friend gave me these. Later, it was easier to remember things because I started writing them all down, so obsessed with the internet that my mother would take the keyboard with her when she left me alone in the house in an effort to curb my habit. It didn't matter. I just typed, slowly and painstakingly, with my computer's character map, clicking one letter at a time, wrapping ice in a towel and placing it on the PC's tower, so my mother wouldn't feel its warmth when she came home and touched it, hoping to catch me out. When my MySpace was wiped, it felt so much like a loss because it was: tracts of my life literally deleted, gone. I'd never remember them again.

These stories make up who I am, form a timeline from there to here, but I don't remember them – not the way you're supposed to remember things, at least. I know they happened because somebody told me they happened and I repeated it all, first to myself and then to other people: to boyfriends and friends, in essays, in therapy. My analyst once asked me what I could remember from childhood: what I could actually *remember*, not what I'd been told had happened. In most of my memories I floated above myself, an objective narrator not involved but somehow still watching, taking on the role of my mother or sister or grandmother, whoever had told me what it was that I'd supposedly done. It felt like I was playing *The Sims*, and just as facile.

I scrabbled for several minutes, looking around the therapy room at things I presumed were there to aid the recovery of memory: a print showing the phases of the moon, a reassuring pile of psychiatric journals, a surrealistic oil painting of a small girl holding a flower. But the exercise failed. The only thing that was really there was the death of my grandfather. When my mother told me he had died, I was so taken aback I laughed. I also remembered a dream I'd had just after my sister left home, my mother turning into a witch and keeping me captive. That was pretty much all I had.

Sometimes I see it happening, feel the thing slipping away from me even as I hold it in my hand. One memory of a lover was so potent to me that I thought about it every day for two months straight. When I stopped for a week, it was gone entirely, nothing but the shape of it remaining. I knew that what had happened had happened in my bedroom, I knew it involved him saying something to me about how I looked, how he felt. But that was it: I hadn't written it down, so it vanished. I couldn't come for weeks.

I always thought it was curious that someone with almost no memory would be so drawn to writing about herself: what material could I possibly have? I knew so little about my subject. But the formalisation of memory – and the formalisation of what those memories meant for me, for who I'd become – was the only way that I could really hold on to them. I'd repeat experiences in my head like prayers, writing and rewriting them in iPhone notes, in my notebook, in pieces of writing that nobody read. The reason I'd forgotten what had been said to me, what powerful combination of words had filled me with desire day after day, was because I hadn't performed the ritual of writing them down, too frightened that they'd lose their impact if I saw them too plainly in front of me. The words themselves were not a spell; it was the context, the electricity between us, the desire I felt and continued to feel, that made them so compelling. I knew they were ephemeral, and this was part of the slightly painful pleasure of it all: he was gone, he probably didn't mean it, he'd never say anything like it again. Nothing could bring the moment back.

To write it down would have been to keep it. But, like the dream about my mother that had haunted me so, it would also have required keeping something captive, too.

Trauma simultaneously erases memory and rewrites it; it highlights the wrong parts, forces you back to that sublime moment of dissembling pain over and over again. It doesn't matter that you can barely remember the moment itself, that you're only dimly aware of what it might mean: your body was there. Your body remembers. 'If we go over this again and again, there's a chance you might remember more,' my analyst told me one morning. He was probably right, but it seemed absurd: I was already there, I was already living the moment every day. It was as if he was pointing out the details of a room while I was blindfolded; 'remembering more' seemed oxymoronic.

Because trauma itself, no matter how dimly held in your mind, how poorly fleshed out, *is* a memory. The nervous system, working as it should, will regulate itself over the course of a day, fluctuations in mood or arousal tending to stay within a so-called window of tolerance. You get stressed when you miss an important train, but you don't panic, don't break down. You can cope; so can your body.

When you're traumatised, though, the body's ability to self-regulate falters. You panic, you sweat, you overreact. Over-stimulated, your fight-or-flight response gets stuck, malfunctions. You miss the train and you're plunged right back into that moment of primal libidinous fear, your body believing it's under threat and your nervous system acting accordingly. Trauma memories are defective in that they're not really memories at all: they're moments, perpetual, inescapable. The moment you miss the train is the moment you were harmed; sitting quietly at home, unthreatened, can be the moment you were harmed; when you're out, when you're having sex, when you're eating dinner or taking the Tube or calling your mum. You don't 'remember' trauma like you remember a date, a story from school, a nice day out; it's something you're inserted into. Or maybe 'plunged' would be a better word.

Perhaps this is why the memories of places are so powerful to me, why being somewhere is the only way, really, I can remember things. To have a memory that isn't fully embodied, that isn't tangible, is alien to me: memory like a headache, like an ache, like a wound. I can't remember what my lover said to me in bed but I do remember where we met; I remember him pointing at me from the stage his band were playing in a huge central-London courtyard one summer night; I remember being in a nightclub afterwards, red ribbon rope lifted just for us. I see the name on the map, on the front of a bus, on a road sign, and suddenly I'm there again: the crushing pain, the thrill and the exhilaration of doing something so desperately, hopelessly bad for me. I'm dumbly reminded of Proust's memory, the madeleines that somehow involuntarily conjure the past. The difference is how desperately I *want* to remember, how fruitless it is when I try.

This wasn't all. There was also my bipolar disorder, which swung me backwards and forwards in time like the hand of a defective clock. Now I was low: I couldn't move, I was lethargic, I was in bed, I was pinned to the floor with anxiety. I was vacant – a chasm, a deep, blank rip in the fabric of time. Now I was manic: empty, still, but in a different way; I was light, I could move my body, and wanted to. Empty, still, but deep in pursuit of things that might fill me up – anything to touch the void, to agitate it. Anything to disquiet, to unnerve. Anything to incite myself to psychic self-violence.

Even now when I think about the ebbs and flows of my mood, I feel distant, at a remove. It feels as if there's some essential 'I' operating from above: not godlike really, but something more primal, an animal self. Something that speaks to the body – a physical body that was the only thing I could guarantee had stayed the same. When I was unstable, the things I desired and the people I liked would change: what I wore, where I'd go out, what I wanted from life. It truly was like I was living two lives. Three, if you count the periods of stability.

And throughout my twenties, it was my bipolar disorder that I used both as an aid to my memory and as a narrative device, a way to root myself in the world. I knew I'd been in hospital in 2015, when I was depressed, so that must have been when this thing happened, when I met that person; a manic spell in 2016 was when I moved abroad because I thought I was in love. Each episode marked a new period of my life. How else would I remember what I'd been doing? There's a level of self-obsession that comes with having a severe mental illness: so used to monitoring your moods, your disordered thoughts, you become fixated on yourself, on who you are and what you're doing and where you've been. At times it felt like I was in a history lesson; the subject was me.

The one thing I never considered was where I'd eventually end up: so preoccupied with my memory that I was facing backwards, so resigned to my frequent bouts of utter despair that I assumed I'd soon be dead. But as I slowly got better, more stable, that changed. I was about to turn twenty-seven when I became obsessed with ageing, and with my own age too. It was never something I'd considered before, an irrelevance, really, except as a tool with which to flirt with older men.

But something changed: a click. I started bringing up my age, almost always unbidden, during random conversations. As if performing a superstitious ritual that might keep them old and me young, I made fun of friends of thirty-three, thirty-four, like the six years between us were cavernous, significant in some way. In the year since the publication of a book that at first I described as 'my first book' and then simply as 'my book' when another one steadfastly failed to materialise, I would stress at any given moment how young I was when I wrote it, as if I'd got a physics degree at twelve or performed improbable sums aged nine on BBC *Breakfast*.

I started to worry that I was 'too old' for things. I measured my emotions carefully, as if I'd discovered there was a finite store of them, that I had to ration them out until I'm eighty-five. Sometimes I secretly hoped I might not age at all, if I might actually be the first person to live for ever.

And death: death rushed at me from every angle. I became preoccupied with my own death, completely obsessed with it – ironic, considering I'd spent most of the prior ten years thinking of increasingly imaginative ways to end my life myself. I'd badly calculated overdoses, my life vomited sharply back up into a toilet I hadn't bothered to clean. I'd wandered into the sea without stones in my pockets, a green and unprepared Virginia Woolf. I'd swayed and wobbled at the edge of a platform, breathlessly hoping for a train to come and crush me, somehow terrified I'd be pushed by someone else at the same time. I'd cut myself, the white-purple-red scars on my arms an artless criss-cross, a child's impotent scribble. Hours wasted online making shopping lists of drug combinations that some anonymous forum member *swore* would finally do it. I was obsessed: death a teenage pin-up whose poster I couldn't bring myself to tear off the wall.

But now it was other people's deaths that seemed to stalk me as I tried to make my way around the world. Watching a ten-year-old boy talk to his grandfather on the Tube induced

physical pangs of torment: *Doesn't he know he's going to die?*
But it was my mother who I reserved as the ultimate object of
my anxiety, turning her mortality over and over in my hand
like a pebble. Every phone call I got felt like a harbinger of
her death, every text from my sister, the twice-yearly emails
from my dad. I felt like the victim of a curse, some doomed
figure from myth. I was the only one who realised we were all
mortal. I was the only one who realised that we were all going
to die.

At first, this didn't seem relevant to my problems with
memory – or at least, it was connected only inasmuch as the
future is always connected to the past. But trauma had trapped
me in the present, left me unable to locate myself in the
world. My faulty memory meant I couldn't find myself in the
past. I knew I'd been there, that it had left its mark on me and
I on it. And yet it was gone: a wisp of hair in a locket that you
can't quite believe was ever alive, was ever part of something
real.

But the future wasn't there, either. I refused to die; I refused
to age. I knew it was one or the other, but neither made sense.
I wanted to live but I didn't know how; despite all the storytelling, all the anecdotes I'd inserted myself into, I had no real
idea what it was like to be me, what that even meant. I had no
memory. Instead, I'd created a mythology.

It was dark when the coach took me back to London, an
abortive stay at my mother's house over Christmas almost over.

We were driving through my home town, the place I grew up, but the only thing that felt familiar was a screen by the driver's seat, a video stream of a camera on the front of the bus showing exactly where we were. It was this uncanny in-between place. I could see where we were out of the window but that didn't seem quite real. Only at one remove did anything seem remotely relatable to me.

Almost everything we drove by had some meaning: past the place I lost my virginity to my first boyfriend, past the club I used to go to with my best friend on Friday nights, past the bar I was banned from at twenty-one. The pubs we were sick in, the chicken shop where I met someone who eventually hurt me, the house of my primary-school best friend, my university halls, the garage forecourt where I'd buy packet sandwiches after nights out, the cash machine where I realised for the first time that I was in my overdraft. It was painful; a rush. I'd spent six days at my parents' house pointlessly trying to remember something significant to take back to my analyst: a scrap of memory from my childhood, a remnant of anything at all. I'd got nothing. This stream of pure feeling was alien; it overwhelmed me.

And I knew I wouldn't remember it later. I knew that if I didn't write it down, I wouldn't remember it later. But my body remembered. My body knew where I'd been, what I'd done, even if my mind didn't, even if I could only access those memories by being thrown back into them, by being forced to live them again.

It would be a lie to say it was enough: how could it be? But it was something: an affirmation, a confirmation, a vow. I don't remember it. But I was there.

The Last Fight

Hazel Gale

Hazel Gale is a former world and national champion in kickboxing and boxing, respectively. Following a burnout in 2009, Hazel qualified as a therapist so she could devote her time to helping others win their own emotional battles. She now runs a private practice in London, and facilitates workshops and digital courses to teach self-awareness and emotional resilience.

APRIL 2001 (AGE TWENTY-ONE)
This dank Soho alleyway smells of piss and beer and feels like foreboding. It's 2 a.m. The neon sign above a strip club makes halos in the rain-thick air around us – a seedy, otherworldly light. Its pink glow seeps down the concrete walls before vanishing into the piles of fag butts and rubbish at our feet.

Christian and I are arguing again but I don't know what I've done. I've asked, he won't answer, and now he's got that predatory look on his face that comes after alcohol and when

I've stepped out of line. I try to walk away but he grabs my
arm to stop me, moving in closer and pushing my back to the
wall. His hand seizes my throat, choking me, forcing me onto
the balls of my feet and preventing me from speaking. Pinned,
I stare at his contorted face and pray for the spell to be
broken. The veins in his neck and forehead pulse. His mouth
has twisted itself beyond recognition, spitting words at me like
weapons. I look at this man – my lover, my partner – and I try
to remember how I ever let it come to this.

We met at a party a year ago, before I started the second
year of my art degree. He was older than me, tall and mus-
cular, with chestnut skin and slicked-back hair like a film star
from the 1940s. To me, he seemed impossibly cool: a talented
painter, witty and dangerously intelligent. I decided then and
there that I had to have him.

Gradually, as the night wore on, the partygoers peeled away
and then it was only us. We sipped whisky, even though I
hated it, and talked about art and other adult things. Every
now and then, he'd give me a look to let me know he was
interested, enough to keep me in the game but not enough to
make me feel like I had won.

He invited me back to his flat. It was immaculate, just like
him. His paintings were stacked on one side of the room, his
living space meticulously arranged on the other. I flicked
through his work as he made us some coffee. The images were
all of women: some of them naked, some not, but all painted
with a sexual tone. There was something unsettling about
them that I couldn't quite put my finger on. These women

looked like they could be strong and beautiful but he posed them in awkward, exposing positions. The work was powerful, I thought. I wanted to ask him about it, but when he came back with the drinks, he insisted I put them away.

I slept in his bed that night but our lips did not meet. He relished the sexual tension and made a point of stretching it out for as long as possible. It went on for months and with every day that passed, my need for him burned deeper. First, he'd let me sleep in his bed but refuse to kiss me. Then, he'd kiss me but refuse to touch me. Next, he'd strip me naked but refuse to bare his own skin. He was always one step ahead, always making sure to keep me vulnerable – just like his painted women – waiting and needing something from him.

By the time I could call him my boyfriend, I was under some kind of stubborn, lust-fuelled spell – so desperate to achieve what I'd set my mind to that I'd lost the ability to question whether I actually wanted it. This all fits my pattern. I don't fall in love so much as charge into combat, like I'm in a battle and I have to triumph. It's only now that I'm starting to see this as a war I cannot win.

Christian has engineered an intolerable fear that lives inside me, and he's made sure he's the only one close enough to soothe it. He's stopped me from seeing friends and I barely speak to my family. The isolation makes that dread feel even more monstrous: a menacing shadow that lurks within, exaggerating every threat. Now, the rest of the world seems too far away for me to break free. Instead, I cling to the faint hope that I'll finally win him over and he'll change. But the longer we play this game, the darker the shadow grows and the weaker I feel.

Some part of me is aware of what's happening, although I do my best to ignore it. Christian is breaking my sense of identity down into helpless, controllable pieces. It feels like he does it for sport, revelling in his power. He's right and I'm wrong. He's big and I'm small. He's the adult and I'm the child.

He said I could move into his flat but then he banned anything that feels like me: my music, my favourite food, the clothes I like to wear. I've stopped making art for my degree because every attempt gets crushed with criticism. If I come home with a new haircut, he just looks at me and shakes his head. 'That's a cool girl's haircut,' he'll say. 'It doesn't suit you. You're not a cool girl.'

At night, I can sense him moving in like a beast of prey and I freeze, hoping to suspend time and escape. It never works. He climbs uninvited on top of my motionless body and pushes his way inside. I don't see this as rape because I don't say 'no'. But I don't say 'no' because I don't feel allowed; speaking is more frightening than letting it continue. So I protect myself in the only way I have left: I turn my head to the side on the pillow where I don't have to see the anger in his eyes and I wait, just outside of myself, until it's over.

I try to believe that my silence justifies his actions: if only I'd speak up, he'd stop. But my voice was the first part of me to vanish and each time I let him in without his asking permission, I relinquish even more of my strength. In allowing him to mould me, I'm letting him teach me that I'm not worthy without correction. And every time I ignore the sense that I'm being made to do or be something I don't want to, I teach myself that I don't have a right to exist.

Somewhere deep down, I know this isn't OK. But I choose not to feel it.

AUGUST 2002 (AGE TWENTY-TWO)

The cruellest thing about any kind of abuse is that it makes you leave your body and then you don't feel safe to climb back inside it again. Numb has become my default. I run from every kind of sensation for fear of feeling the pain I've been hiding. The shadow has grown too big and too dreadful for me to face.

Christian and I break up ten long months later. It should be a moment of victory. I don't take that opportunity. Once again, I'm frozen by fear and shame and the power of his unwinnable game. I lie on the bed in silence and stare at the ceiling, wishing I could take action. Hours pass but I don't say the words I need to say. My mouth won't open wide enough for me to make a sound.

Eventually, I manage to stand up and put my bag together. We're on the fourth floor of a building on a busy Brixton high street. It takes me another hour to leave the flat. I take three steps and then stop, climb down one flight of stairs and then stop. I sit paralysed on the doorstep outside for the longest time. Then I drag myself down the street towards the station, past the Caribbean restaurants and the gangs of weed-smoking teens. I'm not in my body so I don't really know how

I'm making it move. Somehow, I haul myself onto the Tube and all the way across London to my train home, the entire way denying myself the relief that tears would bring.

I stay numb even when I see my family – all of them – waiting for me at the station in Norwich. My picture-perfect nuclear-family refuge. They look so sad and worried as they wait, reaching out to pull me in and make sure I know I'm allowed to cry. But I can't tell them what's happened because I can't bear to show them my weakness. So I don't. Not for a while.

Once back in London, I finish my degree in a haze of dissociation. I grow obsessed with the question of whether it's possible, while observing a piece of art, to catch sight of something truer than the representation. I find myself transfixed by hyperrealist paintings and photographs, battling with the nagging sense that I'm missing something. I start to wonder whether it's the replicating that art tries to achieve – its falsity – that can afford us our glimpses of reality. It seems like the illusion of the imagery is trying to jog me out of a trance and connect me to something deeper. I sit for hours at my computer, alone, surrounded by plumes of smoke and empty wine bottles, trying to intellectualise the hunch that there's more to this world than the way I am experiencing it. But I'm not ready to ask the more personal questions that could lead me to an answer. Besides, Christian's reproval still shouts too loud in my mind. I leave art behind shortly after graduation and seek a job that will help me drown it all out instead.

Now I'm working in a busy bar, which means I can drink

all day long and always feel like it's OK because everyone else is doing the same. I've become an expert in numbing myself with spirits, cigarettes, drugs and sex with people I feel nothing for. Because when you're not inside your body, it's much easier to let others breach its boundaries.

I'm living in my own hyperrealist painting, a fake-real version of the world. My days, weeks and months merge into a blur of high-free highs and hungover lows. I work double shift after double shift, losing myself in the rush of the job and dulling everything in between with substances that either keep me awake or knock me out – all the time telling lies to myself, as well as to everyone else, about the strength I wish I knew how to find.

FEBRUARY 2008 (AGE TWENTY-EIGHT)

Condensation trickles down the graffitied walls of the gym and gathers in pools on the floor. It's busy in here tonight, the air thick with tension and a need for everyone to get things right. This is how it always is with a big fight on the horizon. People are on edge, they hit harder and worry more about little mistakes. Only a few of us will be competing next week, but the excitement is contagious. From beginner to sensei, everyone acts like they're fixing for a rumble.

Like any good knight in shining armour, kickboxing showed up just in the nick of time. I stumbled upon this place three years ago, having followed my latest crush through the door. It didn't work out with him, but that doesn't matter because I've fallen in love with everything that fighting has to offer instead. Here, I feel like part of a community – like I belong – and for the first time I can taste the promise of real strength.

I can still remember the thrill of throwing my very first punch: the thwack of my glove on the pads, the feeling of power as my knuckles connected. It felt like an awakening: a return to my right to battle back and a chance to prove that I'm a woman who can't be fucked with. Finally, I feel like I've found a language to tell the story I need to tell.

Right now I'm training on my own, working on the same big, heavy boxing bag that I always choose. It's comfortably familiar, the right height and weight, with its curves and indentations just where I need them to be. There's a rhythm to this kind of practice that offers an intoxicating sense of certainty. I work hard to lose myself in the repetition of my favourite combinations, relishing the power I've taught my body to own. Hard and heavy hands followed by the satisfying thud of shin into leather. And repeat. And repeat. And repeat.

The beeping timer signals the end of my round, and I pause to watch two men sparring in the ring next to me. They move with an intensity reserved only for combat sports: eyes cold, focused and shark-like, fists poised to punch, knees twitching, ready to lift a leg and strike. To train as a fighter is to unlearn your natural instincts. You have to condition yourself to keep your eyes open while under attack, to move forward into risk rather than flinch and shy away, to fight when you want to freeze. It takes effort to fine-tune these most unhuman of skills but it's what I have to do. If I want to win the battles I walk willingly into, this is what it'll take.

One of the men, a forward-moving fighter, ducks under a hook and counters with an uppercut that lands flush. The other man's nose starts to bleed, dripping onto his shirt and the floor beneath them. Still breathing heavily, I gaze at their feet as they dance red all over the canvas and my thoughts drift to the competition.

In the world of fighting, my ability to numb plays a crucial role. It's a big advantage to be outside of your body when you're trading blows. You need a way not to feel the discomfort of both being struck and striking another. I use my extra distance to power through the sparring, the press-ups, the sprints, the bruises and the cuts, quite literally hardening my outer shell and fortifying myself. I've earned the right to fight for this title. This is how I'll shake off the shadow of weakness for good.

The men in the ring are putting on the perfect display, moving like wild animals in their voluntary cage. I observe them with intent, as if I can absorb their skills by osmosis. I fantasise about my own devastating counters and dancing feet, my own punches drawing blood and that moment of glory when the medal will be hung around my neck. Victorious, at last.

The daydream is interrupted by a tap on my shoulder. I'm needed in the office, apparently. Throwing my gloves to the side, I walk away from the still-swinging bag and towards the front of the gym. I keep my chest puffed out as I stride through a class of red-belts learning the basics, making sure to flash them as big and confident a smile as I can muster.

My coach sits behind his desk, surrounded by trophies and title belts: a very literal display of his worth. They glisten and shimmer under the low lighting, intimidating and inspiring in equal measure. Coach has a fighter's face with a flat nose and deep-set eyes. Today he's in sweat-soaked training gear and a baseball cap, with the usual nonchalant air about him – the kind of calm authority you can only enjoy when you're the undisputed king of the heap. He's just a few years older than me but I think of him as my fighting father figure and I feel honoured that he's chosen to mentor me for this competition. I can't wait to walk to the ring with him by my side. He doesn't do that for everyone – least of all the female fighters – so it makes me feel recognised and seen, filling a void that's been too long left wanting.

Squeezing past a stack of piled-up boxes, I look around for somewhere to sit. In lieu of a second chair, I pull up a small wooden stool and crouch down, a little too low for comfort, waiting for my instructions. I never really know what to expect from these coach-to-fighter conversations. I hope for praise but it always feels uncertain. Perhaps it's just an echo of my past, but as I watch him sort through the money from the till, my mind goes searching for something I could have done wrong.

Finally, he looks up. 'I'm not going to be in your corner at this tournament, Hazel. I have other things I need to do that weekend.'

Coach looks back down at some papers while I hover in a state of disbelief, waiting for him to say more, aching for an explanation or a way to change this. But nothing comes, and in the silence the sting of betrayal cuts deep. This man, my father figure, is the only person I really want to be at the competition. In fact, right now, it feels like he may be the only reason I'm doing it.

Anxiety sears through me as my mind floods with images of me fighting without Coach close by, stripped of his support and validation. The idea of that glorious ring entrance fades, my dancing feet along with it. Instead, I see myself caught off guard by a brutal flurry of punches, getting schooled by an opponent who's fitter, sharper, better than me.

Over the last few years, I've come to pride myself on being able to resist the feeling of fear. But now that same old shadow begins to rumble within. It's the ultimate sign of my weakness and I've done all that I can to get away from it. I've taught myself to laugh off my nerves, train them off, fight them off, channel them into power. But this news penetrates the shell of my fake-real strength. The words growl and thunder through my body, wrapping themselves around my throat from the inside and freezing me motionless. All over again, I'm back in that alleyway with Christian, unable to say or do anything other than wait for him to release me. But Coach is focusing on something else now. The conversation is over.

The following week, I travel out to the championships with the rest of my team. By now, I've let the pain of that rejection evolve into anger in the hope that I can find some strength in fury. I want to prove that I can win without Coach telling me what to do, as if my victory will put him in his place. But beneath the bravado the fear is back, stealing away the confidence I thought I'd reclaimed, urging me to check out.

We walk into the sports hall trying to look poised and set up camp near the boxing ring. To weigh in, we have to strip to our underwear and queue up for the scales in full view. I'm vaguely aware of the thought that this should be humiliating but I can't find the will to care. They can look all they want.

By fight time, I've detached completely. I'm not in my body. I'm not even in the room. I find a substitute coach to warm me up and walk me out. Then, he stands in my corner with the towel and spit bucket, shouting instructions and cheering me on. He applauds as I dominate my opponent, forcing her onto the ropes with the combinations I've taught my body to throw so well. Hard and heavy hands followed by the (un)satisfying thud of shin into ribcage. And repeat. And repeat. And repeat.

As the medal is hung around my neck, I search for the sense of completion that I've been working towards. But just like my break-up with Christian, this victory feels empty: abstract and climax-free. I'm too far away from myself for any of this to land. Even though I'm officially declared the best, the strongest, the fastest, I'm not able to feed that power to the shadow because she still can't open her mouth wide enough to consume it.

This, it turns out, is just another fake-real version of my story. A little too strong. A little too proud. A little too perfect.

I've been fighting as often as I can, winning some and losing others, desperately striving for a victory big enough to believe in. When I lose, I feel so exposed it's unbearable, as if for one dreadful moment everyone can see the real me: fragile and easily breached. These defeats threaten a rupture so unacceptable I guard myself in every possible way. I stop friends and family from coming to watch me and distance myself even further by stubbornly sticking to the lies that I'm telling.

Gradually, though, the falseness of all this is starting to erode the shell and my once-strong body is breaking down. I grow sick with fatigue and begin to burn out hard, but even this can't keep me from training. The need to feel strong and productive outweighs everything else, and striving for my own collection of shimmering trophies feels like the only way to satisfy it. I rack up title after title – British, European, World – each one stealing a little more of my health and none of them quenching my thirst. No matter how much damage I'm doing, I can't stop.

Then, one day, I receive a phone call from my mother. Somehow, even before she speaks, I know what she's going to say.

'He's gone.'

My dad died of a heart attack this morning, right in front of her. He was gone before they reached the hospital. There was no warning, just a look of confusion on his face before he fell to his knees. I can see this image in my mind as if I had been there with them. I know the expression he would have had. I know the way he would have fallen. Silently, I listen to my mother's drawn and distant voice as she says the words that no one ever wants to have to say.

I put the phone down and sit watching the wall in my empty flat, willing myself to move. I want to get home as fast as I can so I can see my family – all of them – waiting for me at the station, reaching out to let me know I'm allowed to cry. But there is no more nuclear-family refuge. Dad's departure has detonated the bomb, shattering my almost-picture-perfect reality into oblivion.

A friend drives me back to Norwich. I ask to stop on the way so we can buy wine and cigarettes, as if these old coping mechanisms have the slightest chance of saving me. When we arrive, I find the ghosts of my mum and my younger sister at the kitchen table. They both look up and right through me. I join them and sit with my head in my hands, staring at the grain of the wood and wondering how life can ever continue without him.

In the weeks that follow, I want more than anything to escape my feelings, but I can't. I keep expecting to have those mornings when you wake up having forgotten what's happened and it takes a few blissful moments before the reality hits you. But the truth of Dad's death is so present that it stays with me all night long. I'm aware of it at every possible moment, sleeping or awake, moving or still. There is no respite.

The strangest thing is that, amid all the shock and confusion, something finally feels real. I'm not talking about everyday reality. That feels weird as fuck. But the agony I'm experiencing is truer than anything I've ever known. This puncture is too deep to pretend it hasn't happened. It's a rupture so fundamental that I have no choice but to stare into the abyss. And what I find – when I do – is all the hurt and fear that I've been fleeing for so long, concentrated and inescapable.

One night, lying sleepless in bed, I find myself turning a strange and distant memory over and over in my mind. It happened when I was about twenty, before Christian and before fighting. We were in a pub with my sister, who was shy and timid then. Dad insisted that she go to buy the drinks because he wanted her to build her confidence. I watched her walk reluctantly over to the bar, and when I turned back to him, he had a sad look on his face. 'Sometimes,' he said, 'I worry that I've failed you both as a father. I wanted you to grow up strong and independent, so I was tough on you, like my dad was on me. But then I worried I'd overdone it, so I went easier on your sister. Now I'm afraid that I overdid that too. You're so hard and she's so soft.'

It's not that this memory has only just come back to me. I've thought of it many times, but something about this pain is causing me to read it differently. Losing my father makes me feel like the best part of me has been sucked into the void. It's like an annihilation of everything I can be proud of and this secondary death exposes the lie that I've been telling for decades: that what I've been calling the Self was forged solely of what I thought was required of me by the Other.

Dad's death has ripped away my faithful facade and left me wondering who I am and what, if anything, has ever been mine.

The game, finally, is up.

DECEMBER 2013 (AGE THIRTY-THREE)

The referee checks my hand wraps, as they always do when a fight is over. Then he stands between my opponent and me while we wait for the judges' verdict. I can see my training partners in the crowd, including my best friend, who flashes me a smile. I boxed well today to win this title. I've never felt so present while fighting. Finally, I've learned how to climb back into my body and take control from the inside. Today is the day when I'll realise just how far I've come.

It happens in one sweet moment. As the ref raises my hand in victory, for the very first time I feel strong. But it's not because I've proven myself dominant over another. This prize is the result of the battle I've won with myself. It's the kind of strength you can only feel when you've had to brave the shadow and embrace all that you are rather than all that you wish you were.

I've had to grapple with a difficult truth: that my struggle against weakness dates back so much further than that one abusive ex. For years I convinced myself that I was fighting to prove that women can be strong and that I was finally becoming a person who couldn't be frozen or silenced by the power plays of misogynistic others. That was just my own macho lie. Soft and girly has always been off-limits. As a child, I refused to wear skirts or dresses. I chose power tools over dolls and teddies, rough-and-tumble over tea parties and princesses. I made my father's values my own, learning to overwork like he did and to prize intellect, physical prowess and winning. It was right at the very beginning that I forged my shell of fake-real strength by taking his warning too literally. I rejected anything from myself and from others that didn't fit that shell, and later filled my world with aggressive men because they represented all that I thought I had to be. I defined myself through and for the men in my life, all of my life. And, as a result, I became a caricature of broken masculinity.

But Dad's death meant I had to go searching for the softer, scarier things I'd always refused. I had to find them because it was those parts of him that I wanted to remember, and those were the parts of me that I needed in order to grieve.

And so, bit by bit, I'm learning how to step into my own shadow and see it for what it really is: nothing but hand-me-down shame from a long lineage of people who misunderstood the true meaning of strength. I've been encouraging myself to pause and feel rather than fight and deny; to reach out rather than shut down. Hardest of all, I've been teaching myself to speak when I feel frozen. I know that reaction now as a gift, rather than a curse. Frozen is an instruction. It's what happens when something important needs to be said. I wonder if Dad had also felt frozen when he spoke his truth that day in the pub. If only I'd known then how much more courage that must have taken than hiding in the shadows of his own fear.

As my name is called out over the loudspeaker, I begin to cry. This is the first time I've allowed any emotion in the boxing ring. Instead of hiding it though, I look out into the crowd, search through their cheering faces and imagine my dad among them. I can see him tilting his head to one side and looking at me through glistening eyes, the way he always did when he felt proud. I never let Dad watch me fight because I was too afraid that the cracks would show. Now, with his ghost in the audience, I can feel the pain of that regret. I'd give anything for him to see me, here and now, like this. Not victorious, but vulnerable and real.

Is it possible that I feel closer to him now than I did when he was here? Maybe. It took until this fight – my last fight, almost – for me to understand what he had tried to teach me all those years ago. Hardness, dominance, victory, winning: these things were never required in the first place. My dad knew all along what it took his death for me to learn, the truth that would have brought us closer than we ever were, the truth that eventually taught me how to love and be loved. He knew it and he taught it. It's just that I chose not to feel it.

The Lily Show

Lily Bailey

Lily Bailey is a writer and model who suffered from severe obsessive compulsive disorder (OCD) into her teens. She kept her illness private until the widespread misunderstanding of the disorder spurred her on to write her first book, Because We Are Bad: OCD and a Girl Lost in Thought. *Lily lives in London with her partner Josh and their dog Rocky.*

still though, it didn't make any sense – time didn't work like that. It was unnatural, it was just wrong, it was fundamentally unscientific ... On the one hand: my father, in faded Calvin Klein boxers with a hole over the right butt cheek, kneeling on the kitchen flagstones in February, dustpan and brush in hand, going at the floor at a hundred miles an hour. The hair on his head and Saturday stubble was, let me be emphatic about this, salt-and-pepper-coloured.

On the other hand: the dark black hairs all over the tiles.

Next to him, a leather-bound trunk studded with brassy circles down the sides that he'd brought up from the cellar, initials I.B. stamped on it in black ink. See, he said, this was my school box, it contained everything I needed, from sweets and stationery to gym kit and oh—

also it contained my razor. It had slipped out of a discoloured cloth bag and split open with a crack when it landed on the floor. Big black thing, kinda resembled a microphone, but the top had three silver circles that looked like flying saucers for ants or something – that was the bit that had popped off – and out of it had spilled literally hundreds of short dark hairs.

That's my fifteen-odd-year-old stubble, he said; he was laughing, he sighed. He told me to get the dustpan and brush.

Old hair goes grey, which is why when Dad shaves now he speckles the sink silver with little hairs that look like iron filings. There's no way that hair can be fifteen years old, I should say, because it looks like it was shaved this morning off the face of a man a lot younger than *you*.

I don't say that, just hand him the dustpan and brush from under the sink and then sit twisting my fingers under the chair and filling with this not-nice feeling, and then more than filling: I am *overflowing* and I have to leave the room

because ever sat in a café and become aware that the radio is playing down low and you wonder if it was on all along or if someone at the counter only just switched it on and now you're tuned in to it you can't ignore it and you wonder how you ever did before

That is the feeling.

Like, duh, something's obviously majorly wrong with the world and how can I have lived for ten whole years and not have noticed it before

because Dad wouldn't lie so if he says the stubble is fifteen years old then it is, but also how can it be when fifteen years later the hair on his face is grey and then the hair that doesn't even have the advantage of being connected to a replenishing life source is black black black.

When things exist that can't exist, then that means that the bigger thing they are in is not real, for instance when you watch a TV show with magic in, it can feel real but really everyone is just pretending.

and it's still here nineteen years later, it's in the knickers I haven't been able to throw away for two years because I got my period in them and put them in the laundry basket and when I came to wash them the next day, there they were scrunched in with the dirty clothes I wore yesterday, entirely clean.

It is excruciating to ask everyone in your home – even the men!!! – if they washed your bloodstained knickers and put them back with your dirty clothes to trick you, but these are the things I must do in the name of research.

Anyway, everyone said no, I did not touch your knickers, Lily, so the problem remains that something happened that could not happen in a world that follows physical laws and makes any kind of sense. I call these things glitches. I hold them up to the light and squint through them trying to discredit them so I can believe that things are really real. For instance, of course now I am grown up I know that my dad having black hairs in an old razor and grey hairs on his chin is not incompatible with the sensible order of things.

But months after that my dad and I were driving along the M25 in summer and I saw a Ford Fiesta with snow on its roof, and I said Dad, did you see that car with snow on its roof, and he said no, of course there isn't a car with snow on the roof, it's 30 degrees out here

and I know you won't believe me, you'll believe him or you'll think that I imagined it or made a mistake because really it was just a white roof box or something. And that *incenses* me, that you think I'm lying or confused, because there was snow on that car's roof, there absolutely was.

Also, when I was at school my English teacher showed us *The Truman Show*. She wheeled the TV in on a plastic table right up to the front of the class and everyone was fist-pumping under the desks and whispering 'yeeeesaaah!' because this meant that we wouldn't have to do any actual work in the lesson. Probably I was pleased too. But I was definitely not pleased when the film started because the film is all about a guy going about his business in his day-to-day life until one day he realises that all the people always react to him in exactly the same way. So then he tries to do stuff they won't expect to get different reactions from them and he discovers that they are all actors and actually he has lived his entire life on a film set and his life is just an entertaining experiment that gets broadcast as an evening show on all TVs across America.

So then I started to wonder if I was in my own *Truman Show. The Lily Show.* And I started acting like Truman Burbank and trying to surprise people by doing things they wouldn't expect, like spraying aerosol into the smoke detector at school for thirty seconds to see if all the actor students and teachers would be on set to come out when the fire alarm went off if they weren't expecting it. Because it was an unplanned event so maybe they would be on their breaks somewhere through a door in the sky I couldn't see and they'd all have to come tumbling back through, their half-drunk coffees in one hand and scripts in the other, to get in line for the fire register. But all that happened was that I made myself quite unpopular for a while. I urgently needed to *pull my socks up* and *get my head on straight* or my life was going to go *down the pan.*

Another time when I was on the Tube there was a blonde woman in a tweed two-piece suit and kitten heels, leaning against the door watching a TV series on her phone. Every time something funny happened, she would do this little secret laugh to herself, pursing her lips like a drawer closing, till they disappeared entirely and her mouth was just a black line like a child would draw. Like the actors in the series were her personal friends making a joke just for her. Like she wanted to look like she was swallowing her laugh so people wouldn't see but that *actually* we would see and know just how much fun she was having.

I felt myself getting annoyed, I wanted to shake her and tell her to stop overacting, you're a terrible actress, then I had this thought about pushing her out the train when the doors opened, to see if the crew would come running. The thought made me feel sick because even if she's an actress she's still a person when she's not on set and so then I knotted my hands tightly behind my back and moved several steps away from her.

I was worried I might do something terrible and dangerous so I tried to *snap out of it* by telling myself that films require budgets of millions of pounds and that's just for a few months, so imagine how many millions it would require to run a movie set for your whole life, and are you really so incredibly narcissistic to think that someone is going to invest that sort of time and money on *you*? Don't you think they'd pick someone a little more *noteworthy*?

But anyway I'm getting distracted because I'm trying to tell you about how it's still here *right now*. So two years ago there was the case of the mysteriously vanishing period stain but somehow that felt sort of manageable. What does not feel manageable at all is trying to sign into iCloud and

Your Apple ID or password is incorrect
Your Apple ID or password is incorrect
Your Apple ID or password is incorrect

which is totally ridiculous because I'm using the password I've used for the last ten years, HarryPotter82, so how the hell can it be incorrect?

Unless someone changed my password. That must be what has happened. Someone has hacked into my iCloud and is fucking with me. Maybe the viewing figures on *The Lily Show* went down so they're creating some drama to see what I do next? They're trying to send me mad for the ratings and that's not even an unreasonable thought since that's basically the rules of *Big Brother*.

So *maybe I'm just that narcissistic.*

I change the password. But then I type in the new password and still

Your Apple ID or password is incorrect

and now this makes *no* sense, because that means as soon as I changed my password someone must have changed it again so I wouldn't know it and oh my god, it's all true after all, I am living on a set and I am totally alone

which is how I come to spend 1 hour and 14 minutes under the duvet on the phone with a Scottish man called Colin on the Apple helpline. He assures me that it just isn't possible for someone to hack into your iCloud, it's so secure that this isn't a thing that happens. Have you checked if your Caps Lock is on? Did you type the email in wrong? OK, so we cannae explain why your old password wasnae working but maybe you got so worked up that you messed up a letter when you were typing in your new password so now the password you think you've set isn't the same as the one you *actually* set

and eventually I say OK Colin, thank you, Colin, I should go now, I've taken up enough of your time. And Colin says goodbye, Lily, I hope you get some sleep.

But I call back two minutes later because the initial question of how the password I've always had got busted is nagging and I need something more than *maybe we just cannae explain that bit, maybe we just cannae explain that bit, maybe we just can't cannae explain that bit.* And I hold on the line and finally when I get through I say please, can I speak to Colin and the person I'm speaking to gets a bit shirty and says they don't take requests for specific call handlers and when I press it he says do I know how many people work on the Apple helpline and he's never met anyone called Colin. So I try to explain the situation to him but he isn't Colin and he thinks I'm insane. I hang up.

I cannot cry and anyway what is the point of being sad? Sadness is something like mourning the loss of happiness and how can I mourn something that never really existed? So I am just here with a headache so bad my eyeballs feel like marshmallows on sticks roasting over a fire. I drenched my sheets in sweat but the sweat turned cold very quickly so now I am shivering and cold, and it makes me think of being very small and waking up because I wet the bed. And maybe hundreds of thousands of people were watching me wet the bed when I was five, on *The Lily Show*. And maybe they wondered if I'd try and change the sheets by standing on my tiptoes and pulling the clean linen down from on top of the boiler or if I'd wake my parents and tell them what I'd done. Maybe they voted on it and whichever answer got the most votes determined what I did do.

There's a thought so horrible I have to run to the bathroom and be sick. I'm on my knees gripping the toilet seat, the digital clock by the sink blinks 4:08. Outside the sky is a mulled pink and the birds are starting to sing. Are they watching me now? I wave at the wall slowly. Maybe they have an all-night channel where people who can't sleep tune in and someone who's just finished their night shift and sat down on their sofa with a Chinese takeaway has switched on their set for company. Maybe if they see me waving they will know that I know and they'll decide it's only right to put me out of my misery; they'll smash through the set walls and rescue me. But this is assuming it's people watching the show. Maybe I am entertainment for another species and I'm a funny creature to them, like a Womble or a Clanger. Maybe they think I'm cute. Maybe in their toy shops there are stuffed versions of me that they buy at Christmas for their alien children with four heads. But if they have four heads then probably their days of religious significance are different too.

I think I fall asleep on the tiles because when I next open my eyes the clock says 6:04. If only I could sleep more and avoid the truth. But now that I know something I must know it all; I'm a detective, I must be brave. If someone changed my password, they would have to sign into my email account. I go back to my room and turn on my laptop because I want to know if Hotmail has an activity log and I can see if someone was on my account between the time when I changed my password and the time when the new password didn't work. Because that's when there must have been someone somewhere waiting to hack in and beat me to typing in the new password.

But Hotmail has better.

Hotmail has a section that lets you see all the IP addresses your account has been activated from. And then I find a website that translates IP addresses into locations. All the locations accessed between the ten-minute window of 00:52 and 01:04 are mine.

Everything is still for a few seconds. I can feel my heart beating in my fingertips. Is this enough? Maybe now I should just know it's all in my head and everything is as it should be. Am I relieved? Except ... what about the initial password change? Why didn't HarryPotter82 work in the first place? I will have to check all the IP addresses from the last 24 hours. The map on the location translator website zooms from out of London back in somewhere over Oxford for an email access at 16:07. Oxford!! Oxford?!!!! I knew it, I knew it. I'm being well and truly fucked with. I'm going to, I'm going to—

Oh. I remember I was in Didcot yesterday for work and I used the Wi-Fi in Costa to check my emails. Didcot is very near Oxford and Google tells me IP addresses can be slightly out. I carry on doing the IP searches for the rest of the day. Everything seems OK. But what if I missed something? I end up doing all the IP searches and translations thirty-nine more times. Maybe I should do the whole week? Just to see? Because there would be crew maintenance at any time, so why not just go the whole hog. There are a couple more Oxford moments but then I work out where I was. There's one location near Weybridge I cannot account for. I google *can IP address locations be wrong?* Long story short, yes, sometimes. So maybe I'll do the rest and come back to Weybridge?

But seven days is a long time to check so maybe I should

do it all twenty-four times just to see. After that I spend some time changing my Hotmail password to increasingly complex strings of numbers and letters while checking the IP addresses for changes. *IP addresses can be wrong.* But still, what about Weybridge?

Then somehow a few days seem to have gone by and I haven't left the house. Instead I am carrying around sheets of A4 with hundreds of passwords written all over them, spiralling all around the page and crammed in at the corners and at different angles like a map of an overpopulated city. I am certain that at some point I will catch someone using a strange IP address that cannot be accounted for. Except, except—

The crew have total control so they could just delete the IP addresses they accessed things from immediately after doing it. Or maybe IP addresses aren't even a real thing off set.

So then this whole exercise was a waste of time. What shall I do? What can I do? It's like I have to choose. *Maybe I'm just that narcissistic.* Or, *maybe we just cannae explain that bit.* But not both, you can't have both. I am dialling a number I know too well. I remember pills I took before, pills that made me slow and took away my desire to do things but most importantly, they brought the fog. It is pretty amazing, I am thinking, the level of detail in this production. How I could call any number and there would be an actor on the other end of the line waiting to pick up or hold music programmed or voicemails with different accents and options so I don't get suspicious. But maybe it's not that amazing, not compared to the skill that goes into set mountains and spiderwebs and puddle reflections and the people who play my family and friends. The ache of their loss is the worst. It's like when you're little and you slam your fingers in the car door, but in this case time has stopped at the moment where your fingers are stuck

Hello, Wimbledon Surgery?

Hi, I'd like to speak to my GP?

Can I ask what this is regarding?

I need to go back on my medication.

Putting you through.

Beep beep, beep beep.

So I never solve it. I let myself down. It hurts too much and I choose to be lazy. Give me pills, give me the fog. Don't let me think.

Maybe we just cannae explain that bit.

ADHD and Me

Rory Bremner

Rory Bremner is widely regarded as Britain's top satirical impressionist. As himself, he has been a presenter, writer, quiz-show host, actor, translator and even (briefly) ballroom dancer. In a TV career of over thirty years, Rory has won numerous awards, including three BAFTAs for his long-running Channel 4 satire series Bremner, Bird & Fortune. *In his spare time (as if) he translates operas and plays from French and German.*

I call it my best friend and my worst enemy.

Worst enemy because it's not fun to be disorganised, to take on too much, to begin tasks but not complete them, to be distracted, to lose concentration easily, to not follow instructions. Best friend because it allows me to make the random connections, leaps of logic or imagination that let me live by my wits, see analogies and come up with ideas, puns and punchlines. (And actually, you know what? Sometimes it *is* fun to be disorganised, take on too much, begin tasks, etc., etc. Just not *all* the time.)

Welcome to my world, the world of ADHD – attention deficit hyperactivity disorder.

And straight away, right there, I question the terminology. Attention *deficit*. The implication that you're not paying attention – or at least, not enough attention. In fact, in my experience, I *am* paying attention – just not to the thing I'm supposed to be paying attention to. I'm paying attention to too many things: my surroundings, the people next to me, the siren on the ambulance in the distance, the phone vibrating in my pocket. That's not attention deficit, it's attention *surfeit*. A sense of being overwhelmed, of the mind racing ahead, or sideways; a kind of chaos, often a chaos of delight.

I'd also question the word *disorder*, by the way. It's a condition, fair enough, and sometimes a debilitating one – but a disorder?

At this point it should be said that most people have had some experience of what it's like to be overwhelmed, to have too much going on or be pulled in too many directions. Picture yourself in an open-plan office: phones ringing, people barking into headsets, messages flooding your inbox, TV screens flashing breaking news on the wall. And you're up against a deadline, trying hard to focus. Are you likely to produce your best work in these conditions? I doubt it. Yet for a child in a classroom who has ADHD, this is all too often what daily life feels like.

We all have moments when we're disorganised or simply trying to do too much. The difference with ADHD is that this is the norm, not a temporary aberration. It's when the sense of being all over the place starts to impair your ability to hold down a job or have a stable relationship, when it wears away at your confidence and self-esteem, when you constantly feel frustrated and misunderstood, that you might acknowledge you need help.

In my own case, it was when a relative of mine was diagnosed with the condition a few years ago that I recognised many traits we had in common. Suddenly a lot of things in my childhood made sense. The forgetfulness and disorganisation (my mother called me 'scatty'); the impetuousness – I once tackled our own centre forward in a football match because I wanted to score a goal (I missed); the tendency to blurt out in class or interrupt.

Sometimes I want to go back through my life and apologise to the people I've annoyed – the classes I disrupted at school, the university seminars I monopolised because I hated gaps of silence and felt the need to fill them. But I realise that's just who I was – and in any case, those past acquaintances I've spoken to say I wasn't really that bad. It's simply that in my recollection I was worse and I beat myself up about it.

That's one thing not to do, by the way – beat yourself up about ADHD. It's what makes you who you are and in many ways that's not a bad thing. There are many singers (Justin Timberlake, Robbie Williams), performers (Zooey Deschanel, Lee Mack), athletes and Olympians (Michael Phelps, Simone

Biles), comedians (most of us, Lee included) who identify with ADHD. Far from eradicating the gene as detrimental, nature actually selects for it. 'We're needed,' the great Professor Eric Taylor, doyen of ADHD research, told me. 'We're the ones who eat the poisoned fruit.'

Usually it's not a question of *curing* the condition but of managing it. Realising that it's an inherent – indeed, an inherited (in most cases) – part of you. It's about understanding yourself, finding a job or a lifestyle where ADHD is an advantage. In my case, performing – doing imitations, working as a stand-up comedian – was a natural extension of my teenage irrepressibility. Impetuousness is a valuable, even essential, part of a comedian's psyche. If you don't have a filter, you'll get to the joke quicker; your brain won't repress the instinct.

This was brought home to me neuroscientifically when studying brain images with Professor Katya Rubia of King's College London. If you look at the brain scan of a 'typical' nine-year-old, you'll see areas of the brain – specifically the anterior cingulate cortex – that are already mature. Look at the brain of a nine-year-old with ADHD and these same areas are noticeably underdeveloped, like a jigsaw puzzle with half the pieces missing. Crucially, the lagging parts regulate impulsivity and inhibit inappropriate responses – essential abilities in many areas of life. In comedy, though, such abilities are arguably a handicap.

There is a second feature common to those with ADHD that can mitigate the debilitating aspects of the condition: hyperfocus. Just as ADHD-ers tend to drift while doing tasks that do not interest or engage us, when we find an activity fascinating, we can focus on it to the exclusion of everything else, including (a concomitant downside, this!) any sense of time. We can be utterly absorbed and spend hours on something if our brain is stimulated and our dopamine levels high.

I've written here about my own experience and how I've learned to live with ADHD, partly by having a career in which it actually gives me an advantage. But what of the experience of others, especially children and teenagers struggling with an often undiagnosed condition?

Typically the problem manifests in behaviour: hyperactivity, restlessness, impetuosity. A classroom is not an easy environment for these traits, so many kids will find themselves labelled disruptive, their irrepressibility not tolerated. This can lead to exclusion and, in turn, to the danger of getting in with a bad crowd, self-medicating with drink or drugs, and ending up in the criminal justice system: the journey from classroom to courtroom. (Meta-analysis by Susan Young of Imperial College London suggests that at least 26 per cent of those in prison or young offenders' custody may have ADHD.) There is still a stigma attached to children with ADHD by those who simplistically dismiss them as 'naughty children' (so what are adult ADHD-ers, then?) or their family as 'bad parents', which only exacerbates the kids' despair and frustration.

Don't get me wrong: there *are* naughty children and there *are* bad parents, but what we are talking about is manifestly different, and teachers and health professionals should be able to spot that difference. In Sweden, if a child is excluded from school twice, it is mandatory to test them for ADHD, and some municipalities have initiated special teaching regimes for affected children. As understanding of the condition increases and stigma decreases, it may be possible to find ways to educate and inspire these kids, who are often gifted, boundlessly energetic and imaginative.

Meanwhile, treatment used to manage the condition tends to centre on medication, coping strategies and counselling – ideally, a multimodal approach featuring all three. Medication (particularly methylphenidate, sold as Ritalin) still receives bad press even though it has evolved, is subject to greater scrutiny than most other medicines and has proved in many cases to be effective. Instantly, too: I've heard it being described as 'like putting on a pair of glasses'. A friend of mine told me it had saved his marriage, helping him to focus and control the puppy in his head, to be more empathetic and to better manage his work.

I tried medication before a show once, for a documentary, and noticed only that it slowed my reflexes a little, calming me when I actually needed to be stimulated and alert to the ideas cascading in my head. 'In that case,' said a specialist, 'you maybe shouldn't use it for shows, but go back on it when you're doing your tax return.'

The greatest change in attitudes to ADHD will come through understanding. The recognition that a child, a teenager or an adult who has 'a Ferrari brain and bicycle brakes' (as psychiatrist and ADHD expert Dr Ned Hallowell described it once) may not be irredeemably 'bad' but simply different. This is not an excuse for inappropriate behaviour, just an explanation. People with ADHD *will* react differently, behave differently, learn differently. You don't have to explore the condition far before you come across the well-worn Einstein quotation: 'Everybody is a genius. But if you judge a fish by its ability to climb a tree, it will live its whole life believing that it is stupid.'

I recently met a renowned business executive whose daughter had struggled with ADHD. She had successfully graduated from university and become an excellent and loving mother. I asked him how he and his wife had coped with the hard years, the frustration and despair of raising their child. He could have told me of all the battles and the pain, but he didn't. Instead, his reply, in all its simplicity, is still the best advice I've heard. 'You know what?' he said. 'We just loved her.'

III. Striving

No Cure for Life

Julian Baggini

Dr Julian Baggini is the author, co-author or editor of more than twenty books including How the World Thinks, The Ego Trick *and* The Edge of Reason. *The founding editor of* The Philosophers' Magazine, *he is academic director of the Royal Institute of Philosophy and an honorary research fellow at the University of Kent. He has appeared as a character in two Alexander McCall Smith novels.*

You'll laugh. You'll cry. That's life. But how much? Too much? Not enough?

It's tempting to think the answer is surely personal. It simply depends on how emotional you are and what sort of tears life has given you cause to shed. But every society has unwritten rules about what the acceptable range is. My English grandmother's generation were no-nonsense northern working-class types who had little time for expressions of ebullience or despondency. The only emotional expressions they specialised in were rage and anger. My parents' generation mellowed a little but were still more stiff upper lip than gushing emotion.

My own generation straddles a major change symbolised by the very public outpouring of grief at the death of Princess Diana in 1997. Ever since, emoting and empathising have been de rigueur. The old adage has turned into an injunction: you *will* laugh. You *will* cry. And you *will* share both experiences with others.

But the unwritten rules of emotion do not just regulate how much and how publicly we express ourselves. They also subtly tell us which emotions are appropriate and when. One of the most succinct insights I have got into these rules comes from a 165-second clip on YouTube. Oprah Winfrey is interviewing Pharrell Williams about the hundreds of videos people made around the world showing themselves dancing to his 2013 global feel-good hit single 'Happy'. After they watch a compilation of clips, Pharrell starts crying. Never one to turn off the waterworks when there's an opportunity to open them up to full, Oprah then starts talking about his late inspirational grandmother. Hankies are passed. The interview video itself then went on to become a viral hit.

It also made me rethink the so-called tyranny of happiness: the pressure to be happy, because if you're not, it must be your fault. We are constantly being told that happiness *is* within everyone's reach. And we are told that we know how to get it: pick up any number of books on 'positive psychology' and you'll see that if you're miserable, you just aren't completing your gratitude diary often enough, or failing to practise your mindfulness, or insisting on clinging onto objects that don't bring you joy, or maybe just eating too many bad-mood foods and not making enough feel-good endorphins down at the gym.

Pharrell Williams's 'Happy' became an anthem for this relentless positivity. Not only was it unapologetically, innocently joyful, but the way in which people made and shared videos showing just how happy *they* were fitted the trend to display happiness as normal, natural, attainable. The song doesn't so much invite as demand that you clap along if you know what makes you happy and you feel like you want to. And when the whole world, it seems, is clapping along, what on earth is wrong with you if you don't feel able to join in? So far, so 'tyranny of happiness'.

But the narrative wasn't quite right until Williams broke down in front of Oprah. It needed Pharrell's tears to dignify his joy, to save it from shallowness. Yes, happiness can be achieved, but it has to be hard won. It is the salvation we are all heading towards, but first we need to experience what we need saving from.

My miserabilist uncle used to say 'laughing always turns to crying'. In our positive-thinking times, this has become 'crying always turns to laughing'. Not even death can prevent that: your funeral will be not about grieving your death but celebrating your life.

What we call the 'tyranny of happiness' turns out to be something a little more complex. The tyranny is to conform to a certain narrative in which happiness is the end state, but suffering along the way is expected – in some ways, the more the (ultimately) merrier. We kid ourselves we are being realistic because we accept the inevitability of pain and heartache in life. But we're not being realistic at all, because what we really believe is that all the pain will be worth it. We love to hear about people who have triumphed over adversity, who have been through hell but are now blissfully content, bringing audiences to tears with their inspirational stories. We celebrate survivors of cancer or abuse but mostly when they've more than survived. We want to see the ones who have run marathons, climbed Everest or written bestsellers, because that proves to us that everything bad will, in the end, make everything better. We turn Nietzsche's defiant resolution 'what does not kill me makes me stronger' into a simple, descriptive law of the universe.

The endless series of such public testimonies makes me think that we don't just believe in fairy tales, we expect them. The classic fairy tales always involved some unspeakable trial, often in childhood: wicked stepmothers, imprisonment, poisoning, years in a coma, exile, the menace of an evil wolf. Only then could our prince come and everyone would live happily ever after. The power of such fairy tales never came from their particular content. People didn't fear witches or expect princes. Instead, they were cathartic archetypes, ways of reassuring children in particular that no matter what scary things might happen in life, if you do the right thing, *it will be all right in the end*.

Twenty-first-century fairy tales similarly start with awful experiences, often in childhood: trauma, repression, oppression, illness, disability, poverty, depression. Salvation sometimes comes in the form of a prince or princess, but mostly through love, support, understanding, our own sheer grit, a miracle cure or diet. And then we too live happily ever after. The End.

I don't buy it. I could give you philosophical arguments or point to some empirical evidence. But instead, let me fight fire with fire – or rather, anecdote with anecdote, personal conviction and experience with personal conviction and experience. I'll do this on the wager that if you look at yourself and others, you'll find that I'm not the weird one. Everyone's experience is different, but if what I describe to you doesn't ring true, one of us is living in La-La Land.

To start off, it would be helpful to break down the modern fairy-tale narrative into its component elements. The key elements appear to me to be (1) everyone experiences a similar mix of joy and heartache; (2) happiness ultimately wins; (3) those who suffer most always end up appreciating their happiness the most; (4) we can all learn to be happy; and (5) happiness is what we all want anyway.

It would be very nice if all these were true, which is why we are so ready to believe and be reassured by stories that tell us that they *are* true. But fairy tales are for children. Grown-ups who continue to believe in them are not equipped to deal with the real harshness of life. Any benefit they get from temporary reassurance is more than cancelled out by the bewilderment and despair of inevitably discovering that these reassurances are false.

First, take the premise that *everyone experiences a similar mix of joy and heartache*. If you make this claim vague enough, it has a ring of truth: every life contains its ups and downs. But sadly, joy and happiness are very far from being evenly distributed. I have lost count of the refugees who say their lives are so miserable they'd rather die trying to escape them than carry on living in a hell on earth. Many even say this of their own children's lives, believing it's better to risk their death than condemn them to the life they have ahead of them. And the awful truth is that many lose the double-or-quits gamble they take. These people have no redemption.

It may be true that very few lives, perhaps none, contain nothing but misery and suffering. Even in the worst of times, there are moments of temporary relief: transient salvations. But it is very clear that, for some, happiness is but a brief respite, while for others, it is unhappiness that only sometimes spoils a generally very pleasant existence. Most of us lie somewhere in between, but not all cluster around the same point.

This is very apparent in my own life. To date, I have been blessed with more than my fair share of good fortune. Merely to have been born a white man in late twentieth-century Europe gave me a head start on most of humanity. I have been able to pursue my interests and none of my health problems has been especially debilitating. Perhaps most importantly, I am by disposition sanguine, if not cheerful. I have never had to suffer depression, whether you understand the term in its clinical sense or simply as a prolonged period of unhappiness.

However, several people close to me have found life much harder, through no fault of their own. I have relatives who have struggled with depression all their lives. One was left housebound for a long time by his psychological problems and eventually appeared to take his own life, stepping out in front of a truck on a busy ring road. I have lived with someone who resorted to antidepressants and whose two siblings had similar problems. I'm reluctant to describe them as suffering from mental illness because I think the medicalisation of all psychological distress is itself problematic. Depression, addiction and anxiety share some features with physical illnesses but in other ways they are importantly different. This is a controversial topic, far too complicated to go into here. So when I say 'mental illness', it is always in invisible scare-quotes that question rather than disclaim.

These people I have known illustrate some uncomfortable, perhaps depressing, truths. First, not everyone has to go through this. The mantra that anyone *can* suffer from mental illness is true but misleading. It's useful in ramming home the message that these are not usually problems that people bring entirely on themselves and that everyone is vulnerable. But the fact is that some people are much more likely to suffer from psychological distress. Mental illness is not indiscriminate: some are more at risk than others. The same, of course, holds true for many physical illnesses. Cancer can strike anyone but for genetic and lifestyle reasons, some are more vulnerable than others.

Second, for many such people there is no happily ever after. Contrary to the second rule of fairy tales (*happiness ultimately wins*), happiness does not always ultimately win. Some endure a one-off period of difficulty that is overcome. For others, it is a lifelong struggle with periods of respite but no 'cure'. For these people, the happily-ever-after narrative is positively dangerous: when they realise it's out of reach, they are left with no hope.

The third rule of fairy tales, it just isn't true that *those who suffer most always end up appreciating their happiness the most*. Suffering is dreadful, so we are very keen to convince ourselves that it has some pay-off that makes it worthwhile. The most common way we do this is to tell ourselves that suffering gets us to appreciate what we took for granted when we were happy and well. Often that's exactly what happens: there's nothing like a brush with death to put things in perspective. But the cause-and-effect relation is far from reliable or constant.

For instance, if they are honest, people who get a gratitude premium often admit that it seems to come with a time limit. I know someone who wrote very eloquently of how a life-threatening illness made them worry less about trivial hassles and focus on what really matters. But after a few years of it, they were just as peevish and irritated by quotidian annoyances as anyone else. The problem with 'putting things in perspective' is that we can't live our lives as though from a distance. We have to live life from the inside, and what is small in the grand scheme of things can seem very large when it's in front of your nose.

The most striking example of this is the guitarist Wilko Johnson, a lifelong depressive who, already terribly missing his late wife, got a diagnosis of terminal brain cancer. I spoke to him as he was touring under the shadow of his impending death. 'It didn't half make you realise you were alive,' he told me. 'I'm somehow happier than I was before the diagnosis.' However, even by then he had already 'come down from this high, digging everything, thinking, wow, I'm alive'. Later he got an incredible reprieve after doctors discovered he had a rare variant of his cancer that could be treated. But as he told an interviewer at the *Daily Telegraph*, 'I knew I was really getting better from the cancer when I started getting depressed again.' What he called 'the misery' was back.

Also, we just don't hear about the people who don't get any positive side effect at all. I had a relative with a terminal cancer diagnosis. The standard narrative predicts that after an initial shock, they would have rallied and made the most of their last days, finally dying at peace with the world. Not at all. There was nothing but fear from beginning to end, no seizing of any day, no heart-warming reconciliations with estranged friends and relatives. It was a grim end to a troubled life.

The fourth fairy-tale illusion is that *we can all learn to be happy*. I don't doubt for one minute that we can do many things to make our situation better or worse. But the idea that if we would only do the right things everything would be fine is nonsense. Fill out your gratitude diary as much as you like, but that's not going to remove the things in your life that cause you dissatisfaction. Nor can it alter your fundamental disposition, which for many people is rather glum. Other advice is even more useless. 'Get out and see people more!' sounds sensible but if your problem is that you just can't face it, it's as useful as telling someone to head to the reptile house to cure their herpetophobia.

Of course, no one thinks that they are so childish as to believe in fairy tales. The self-deceptive trick we play is to convince ourselves we have embraced imperfection, while all we've really done is embrace imperfection only as a means to a sort-of-perfection. Think, for example, about Brené Brown's TED talk 'The Power of Vulnerability'. You've probably seen it since it's one of the most-viewed videos in TED's history (38 million and counting). Many TED talks are 'inspirational' and Brown's message that embracing our vulnerabilities is the key to becoming fulfilled is just another twist on a familiar theme. What I find most interesting about the talk is that it has a curious double edge. On the one hand, Brown is encouraging people to reject the search for perfection, to have 'the courage to be imperfect'. But on the other, she claims that if we raise a generation of kids to accept this and 'practise gratitude and joy', then 'we'll end the problems ... that we see today'. It's a kind of emotional alchemy, instant karmic payback: embrace imperfection and it loses all its negative power; in fact, it turns out to be good. Brown asks us to learn from the people who believe 'that what made them vulnerable made them beautiful'. Somehow, embracing imperfection makes things almost as good as perfect, after all.

Fortunately, there is a positive-realist alternative to the idea that we can all learn to be happy and that those who suffered most win most. It offers a more modest hope: that life can still have enough of what is worthwhile even for those who find 'happiness' out of reach or only fleetingly graspable. In my experience, people who believe something similar ultimately deal with their problems the best. Freed from the pressure to 'cure' their depression, they come to treat it as an unwanted companion that, managed correctly, can be stopped from ruining everything. They tell themselves, as the title of Whitney Houston's song puts it, 'It's Not Right But It's Okay'.

Think of the 'light at the end of the tunnel'. If everyone tells you there is such a thing but you can't see it, you might easily give up. But waiting for the light to come is not the only option: sometimes it's possible to make the tunnel less dark, and that allows you to live well – if not entirely happily – in it.

Those of us whose friends or loved ones suffer chronic psychological problems need to learn this lesson as well. Too often we try to be saviour figures, a Prince (brother, sister, friend) Charming who will bring the happiness ever after we both want. I have often found myself so keen to avoid 'giving up' on someone that I have persisted with the wrong kind of support, only adding pressure on them to feel better, creating guilt for their failure to do so. I need to remind myself that the choice is not between hanging on to the illusion that everything can be made right or giving up completely. More is often achieved by doing things that make a day or an hour better, even if they don't sort everything out. For example, a dinner with friends doesn't 'cure' depression but a depressed person who takes part in frequent social occasions is rarely as depressed as one with no similar good times. You can offer support but not salvation.

The language of 'mental health' hinders rather than helps in this respect. It is a mistake to assume that all unhappiness or anxiety is a kind of dysfunction. Misery is not a disease to be cured. It is no more sane to be happy than unhappy. Sanity and happiness are completely different things, only weakly correlated. Indeed, the problem many unhappy people have is that they see the truth all too clearly: the world is full of misery, injustice and cruelty, and in the end everyone dies. I sometimes think it is the cheerful who are the most deluded, and we are lucky to have no compulsory corrective for the rose tint we put on our view of the world in order to cope with it.

But perhaps the biggest, most childish flaw of the standard fairy tale is that it assumes *happiness is what we all want anyway*. People often quote Aristotle as saying, 'Happiness is the meaning and the purpose of life, the whole aim and end of human existence.' But the Greek word he uses, *eudaimonia*, is not happiness in the hedonic sense of feeling good. It is better translated as 'flourishing'. We flourish when we lead meaningful lives, ones that enable us to live according to our natures, developing our potential and living well with others. When we flourish, we are much more likely to be happy, but this is a pleasant side effect, rather than the goal.

Happiness is not all that we want because there are other worthwhile goals for a good, flourishing life. The philosopher Arne Næss, for example, talks about 'self-realisation', explicitly contrasting this with feelings of happiness or pleasure. For Næss, this means developing our capacities in the context of things that are greater than us, such as nature. This can bring a profound sense of a life worth living but not necessarily happiness. Think, for example, of human rights campaigners such as Martin Luther King, Jr or Nelson Mandela. They would've hardly been happy working to defeat systemic injustices but they lived deeply fulfilling lives.

The goal here is a life well-lived. One of the starkest examples of such a life was that of the philosopher Ludwig Wittgenstein. He was a troubled soul who, like the proverbial Scotsman with a grievance, could never be confused with a ray of sunshine. Yet, on his deathbed, he said to his doctor's wife, 'Tell them I've had a wonderful life.' Few can live lives as extraordinary as Wittgenstein's, but if at the end of the day we know we have followed the path we truly believed in, as closely as was practically possible, we can all say we have led good and worthwhile, if not wonderful, lives.

Another misquote from Aristotle is that 'happiness depends on ourselves'. Not true, but flourishing does, at least more so than happiness. We have more control over how we live our lives than over how that makes us feel. The biggest single thing we can do to flourish is to focus on valued action: doing the things that we consider, on reflection, to be of value. Do that and your life satisfaction will almost certainly be good, even if you can't shake your blues.

I don't want to give the impression that I find happiness bad and undesirable. All other things being equal, it is certainly preferable to be happy rather than not. But all other things are never equal. If someone is happy right after their child has died, or having luxurious feasts in a castle while all around them people are dying from starvation, we think there is something wrong with them. We don't want to be happy whatever happens; we want what happens to give us genuine cause for happiness. It is only good to be happy when we are happy for good reasons. And sometimes there simply are no good reasons to be happy. Sometimes, the right answer to the annoyingly chipper 'Cheer up, it might not happen' is 'Feck off – it *has* happened.'

However, the main problem with depression is not so much that it keeps you from being happy but that it stops you being anything other than depressed. It induces lethargy and defeatism, which get in the way of pursuing valued action. What many people need most is to do something they find worthwhile, whether or not it puts a smile on their face. Although the tortured artist is something of a cliché, there are certainly artists who have lived wholesome lives while rarely being truly happy.

Wilko Johnson is a terrific example of this. He has had an incredibly productive creative life and gets a great deal out of performing his music. But that doesn't cure the depression. 'As soon as you walk off stage all this sadness floods back,' he told the *Daily Telegraph*'s interviewer. I find it telling that there are countless articles and interviews about how he felt energised by his cancer diagnosis, many more about his seemingly miraculous recovery, but hardly any about how he is now just carrying on, his life a bittersweet mix of thrilling performances and 'the misery'. For a while, his story fitted the fairy-tale template. Once it became clear it wasn't happily ever after, few wanted to hear it.

I don't want to glamourise mental illness. At its worst, it can be harder to live with than most physical diseases. As Johnson describes what happens when his cycle of depression returns, 'You're just going down and anything you think about will bring you down. You lose all energy and enthusiasm for everything. It's horrible.' My point is simply that the solution to depression or anxiety is not always to seek their opposites. The problem is the degree of unhappiness, not the unhappiness itself. The terminally glum can have good lives, potentially better than those of the glibly happy. Once our problems are reduced to a level where they don't debilitate us, life can become as rich and meaningful as it is for anyone else. Unhappiness needs to be put in its place, not denied any place at all. It's not enough to say 'life is often hard'. We have to fully accept that not everyone can be happy or should necessarily strive to be happy. And this means also accepting that since a cure that kills is no cure at all, there is no cure for life.

It Could Have Snowed, It Snowed

Alex Christofi

Alex Christofi is the author of two novels, Let Us Be True *and* Glass, *which was longlisted for the Desmond Elliott Prize and won the Betty Trask Prize. He has spent the last couple of years reading everything that Dostoevsky wrote, and can finally confirm that the ones you've heard of are the best ones.*

My great-grandfather was a murderer. I think about it every time I walk along the beach in Larnaca, which is quite often. My brothers, my father and I have a ritual whenever we return to Cyprus: within a day of arriving, we go to the promenade, Finikoudes, a kilometre-long strip named after the palm trees that line the road. We park our hire car in the Turkish quarter in whatever shade we can find, and then stroll along to one of the kiosks that sell fluorescent souvenirs and ice cream ('Two euros!' they shout in English, and then: 'One euro!' in Greek). We order four toasted sandwiches. The bread has to be covered in sesame with just one or two aniseeds. The filling has to be sliced cucumber, halloumi and lountza, a wine-cured pork loin not unlike bacon. After all these years, the jury is still out on whether to include tomato, which turns to lava under the grill. The sandwich always has to be piping hot – it doesn't matter if it's 40°C outside, that's just how it is.

In order to get to any of the kiosks from the Turkish quarter, you have to walk past the fortress. The building meets the beach and is now a museum. I've never been inside but I've peered through the entrance into the bright courtyard where huge terracotta pots soften the bleak image of the flag-stones. We don't know how long my great-grandfather spent in there; certainly at least five years, but probably not as many as twenty. I don't want to spend a single minute in there, even though I must have walked around it dozens of times. I have leaned against it in the sun and put my hand against the warm stone on cool nights, flushed with the pleasure of a long, slow meal of shared plates and tall glasses of ouzo. It has become a strange kind of gravitational centre, a dangerous one. Skirting close to it seems to lend me energy, but I always have the feeling that if I linger too long, I might get sucked in and obliterated.

The strange thing is that I don't know my great-grandfather's name and I hadn't even realised until I decided to tell it to you. It's sometimes hard to notice the things that aren't there, hard to value them. Think of all the children that were never born. When a young bachelor gets into a fight over nothing and someone throws a brick at his head, all his futures die with him. Up to that moment, the whole untold leap of life could be traced in one unbroken line, countless millions of years from the first tiny primordial swimmers through the birth of teeth, fins, feet, legs, the birth of shelter, invention, art, up to the moment his head hits the earth, when the line breaks abruptly, comes to nothing. Life invented so much and took so long to get here and, after everything, all it took to stop life in its tracks was a bit of stone picked up out of the dust.

My birth, and that of my father, and that of his mother, were contingent on the British colonial law of the time. My great-grandfather was sixteen when the other man died. If he'd been a few months older, he would have been convicted as an adult and sentenced to hang by the neck. Stood on a trapdoor, a leather strap around the ankles, a white hood and a rope knotted at the side of the neck. A brief revolting moment of vertigo as the guards release your arms before the trapdoor collapses. According to the hangman's notes, it would have taken no less than seven seconds and no longer than ten. And after that, I would never have existed.

The details of the crime itself are scant, so I tend to think I must have embellished the story over the years. (Joan Didion put it best in her essay 'On Keeping a Notebook': 'It might as well have snowed, could have snowed, did snow.') Memories are not imperishable, they are organic and there is no reliable way to tin or vacuum-pack them. I squash this fragile lump of memory into new shapes every time I return to it, picking it up, turning it over, setting it down to flatten on a different side. This is what I think I know: that my great-grandfather was a labourer, a farmer or a builder (a lot of my family were builders). He used to work day in, day out, baking away in the sun, stopping only when it bore down with force from above, making all work impossible. Then he would lay down his tools and eat bread and olives under a tree until the shadows stretched and pooled and work could begin again. Barely more than a child, it wasn't so long ago that he and his friends played games together in the square until it got dark, running around or throwing stones at tin cans. He was always the best shot; in fact, he never missed.

One of the other villagers would ride past on his donkey every day, shouting obscenities at him. Perhaps the first day he laughed it off, perhaps he resolved to keep working, glaring stolidly at a piece of masonry in his hand, or a trowel. I have never been told what the insults were, but all insults are the same under the surface: your family deserves no dignity. You are your mother's great mistake. You will have no children. The future does not belong to you. Insults are attacks on selfhood, the part of you that wants to keep living. The only way to answer an insult is to prove that it is they who are mistaken, they who have no future. The decision to kill is the sharp end of the decision that we make every day, the logical conclusion of our society, which assumes we all act in our rational self-interest. Albert Camus put it like this: if forced to choose between justice and my mother, I choose my mother.

The story on my mother's side is no better and possibly worse, depending on what makes you squeamish. My mother's grandfather was very poor but he worked hard to provide for his family. At that time, it was a husband and father's only role, one half of the marriage bargain that governed life's majority. But he fell ill – gravely ill, so that he could no longer work. He had a family to support but no way of supporting them. In his illness, he could not feed his family; worse still, he became another of the mouths to feed. He had only ever been offered one role in life, and he couldn't fulfil it. One night, after the others had gone to sleep, he didn't go up to bed at all, but put the lights out and lay down in the sitting room so as not to disturb them later. I can't believe that he slept. After the long hours, before dawn, he got up and put on his Sunday suit. I don't know if he left a note, if it was a full moon or if he walked in darkness.

He went to Poole Park, not far from where I would be born. I used to play there happily as a child, demanding fifty pence from whichever of my parents was in a better mood so that I could have a go on the remote-controlled speedboats. You couldn't go far on them and you weren't allowed to crash them, but I dimly understood that they represented freedom at a time when I hadn't connected speedboats with money and still assumed that some families in Poole had yachts because they really liked yachts, whereas my family preferred picnics. I remember the park had a wide ring of tarmac where I could ride my little pedal-operated go-kart (or push my older brother around in it when it was not my turn). The beauty of riding around a ring for a parent is that the karts are only getting away from you for so long. The further they travel, the closer they are to coming back to you.

The park also has a wide lake. I can't recall anyone ever swimming in it. The way I remember it, Poole lake was not a glorified pond but a domesticated sea, flat enough to ride a pedalo but big enough that it seemed to generate its own wind. Swans would bring up their cygnets there and teenagers would learn to windsurf, heaving themselves up and away from the opaque slate-grey water. Now I think to myself: the water is cold; the water is where life began; the water is where we forget ourselves. Back then, I liked to go to the lake and if I thought about anything at all, it was whether we would be given money for the speedboats, or whether we would simply play with the lifeless remote controls and imagine the boats were moving.

I don't know what my mother saw there, if it brought to mind a sickly man with his Sunday best hanging off him, collecting stones to put in his pockets, finally resolving to dip a polished shoe into the cold water. It seems cruel to ask, partly because that suffering bears so little relation to my happy childhood. What is most striking to me is that I feel no ownership over that man's suffering, the overwhelming pain that must have driven him to suicide, even though he did it all for me – or for the idea of me. Life had broken its promise to him and in the absence of justice, he chose, or believed he was choosing, to spare his children.

These two choices – murder and suicide – were the product of two very different societies, one policed by honour, the other by guilt. The guilty society keeps its esteem locked up in its heart and puts on a suit and tie to walk along the bed of a

lake. In the honourable society, esteem is conferred or with-
held by the village. It would be easy, for instance, to think that
my father's grandfather felt guilty when he killed, but that is
only how I would feel. He might have felt that it was better to
die with an honourable name than to live with a shameful
one, that he would gladly give up the use of his body in a cell
or at the gallows so that his family might walk proudly into
any room. All that it requires is a change of perspective.

I don't know that it snowed on the morning that Fyodor
Dostoevsky was due to be executed for sedition, but it was at
the end of December in St Petersburg, and when I imagine it,
it is snowing.

He was taken with five others to the drill ground of the
Semyonovsky Lifeguard Regiment, which is now a peaceful
park with sycamore trees and a children's playground. As a
crowd of local residents watched, the group were led over to
three posts stuck in the bare ground. They were given white
shirts and blessed by a priest. Dostoevsky couldn't bring himself to believe that they would be executed until a friend
nudged him and pointed to a cart stacked with what looked
like coffins. Three of the men were tied to the posts and blindfolded opposite the regiment, which lined up with their
rifles. The rifles were raised, waiting only on the order to fire.
Dostoevsky was fifth in line. With no more than a minute left
to live, he thought of his brother, Mikhail, and his family, how
much he loved them. Just then, a messenger arrived with a
stay of execution: the Tsar had granted them their lives and

would send them to Siberia instead. Dostoevsky found himself in the jarring position of living on past the date of his own death.

When he returned to his cell after his execution, the first thing Dostoevsky did was write his brother a letter telling him to look after his family. It is perhaps the most ecstatic letter he writes in his lifetime. He reassures Mikhail that he is not worried about hard labour: the task of his own life, as he sees it now, is 'to be a human being among human beings'. He still has 'a heart and a body that can love, and suffer, and desire, and remember, and this, after all, is life'. Looking back, he sees only how much time he wasted, how little he valued time. 'Life is a gift, life is happiness, each minute might have been an age of happiness.' Youth, he writes, is wasted on the young. Which is just as well, as he was about to spend the rest of his youth in Siberia.

When Camus says justice or my mother, it sounds so simple. It seems like a straightforward choice between humane instinct and cruel ideology. It makes me think of those horror stories where Nazi children turn their parents in to the authorities, a dystopia where ideology has crept in under the nails and eyelids, suffocating even the simplest, most natural instincts. To reject that vision seems like the only human choice. And yet here is something I also believe to be true: if you follow racism down to the bitter root, or murder, or even, in some cases, suicide, what you find is preferment. The belief that there is a lifeboat to the future and that you would give up anything, even justice, to make sure that you or your family are on it.

Because we prefer, we privilege; unless it is given away, this privilege compounds itself; the privileged now have something to lose; to desire others' gain, the logic goes, is to desire your own ruin. And so humanity drifts apart. Some grow into a world where, as they stumble, adult hands reach out to catch them. Others only fall a little way, only scrape a knee, learn to be more careful, learn not to make those mistakes again, though there are countless other mistakes to be made. Some people live in a generous world and don't understand why others don't feel generous. Some people don't feel any ill will towards the poor because they don't know much about them and don't find them interesting to think about. Some people eat when they are full. Some people hold wealth so great that it can only be expressed as an abstract value. Some sail out on the lake, while others watch from the shore.

We are all born with a desire to live on – to eat, to have sex, to have children – but we are also desperate to imprint ourselves on the memory of others, to write, to be known, to be remembered. To protect and propagate the self: this is how the world would have us. And if that's all we do with our lives, we are no better than wind-up toys. If freedom, if humanity exists at all, it comes in the decisions we make that aren't simply an extension of our drive to propagate ourselves. (In this view – in my view, I admit – kindness is the only true freedom.)

Hours after the appointed time of his own death, the future of his family vested in his brother, Dostoevsky was finally free.

In his freedom, for the first time he simply wanted to be among others, to be a creature that could love and suffer. We spend our lives imagining that the two are opposites, that the consequence of minimising our own suffering is our own happiness, but here Dostoevsky places them alongside one another. He seems to see suffering not as a spectrum that ends in death but as proof that he is alive. To love is to feel how good it is to be alive; to suffer is to appreciate what it might mean to die.

We all know we need love, but few suffer willingly. Today millions eat opiates, sand down the world's edges and wander uncertainly into a shapeless void. There are a few, by contrast, who see suffering as a tunnel, a shortcut, and they run into the darkness willingly. They kick against the earth thousands of times. In their struggle, they feel sick, their knees hurt, their nipples bleed, and as they reach the far light, when they finally stop running, they can actually feel the world spinning.

What, then, should I make of my family history? It would be simple enough and true enough to say that my great-grandparents' suffering set the conditions for my happiness. That they threw me onto the lifeboat. It's a reassuring conclusion: suffering can lead to happiness. Or perhaps: we are happy because we suffered for a reason. I would go as far as to say that a life devoid of suffering would be a life without meaning. I could leave it there. It would satisfy my narrative impulse to tidy up after myself, to make the story about myself. It could have snowed, might as well have snowed, and so we say it snowed. But I find myself snagged on another, less accommodating truth.

I don't know that I have anything to offer my great-grandparents except that I am alive to appreciate them, to try to understand what they went through. The murdered man, too – even if no one else thinks about him, I do. It didn't have to be me; it could have been someone else in my place. That is the important thing, the little speck in the vast expanse of the universe that knows what it is. The little bubble of order in a swell of chaos. Life has learned to love itself but it has no favourites among its children. People can be so myopic; they peddle difference, they fight, they waste their time asking questions like, 'Justice or my mother?'

The harder I try to impose meaning on it all, the more I am glad simply to be alive, to have a heart and a body that can love and suffer and desire and remember, and this, after all, is life. One man lays his hand on the wall of his prison cell and a hundred years later another lays his hand on the outside, thinking strange thoughts. I am the world experiencing itself subjectively. I am the great-grandchild of the murdered man. I am an 'I' that shouldn't exist, a happiness born out of suffering, standing between the lake and the shore, the fortress and the sea.

The Pilgrimage

Elitsa Dermendzhiyska

*Elitsa Dermendzhiyska is a social entrepreneur working at
the intersection of technology, research and mental health. At
twenty-five, she left her software business to interview
clinicians, nurses, psychotherapists, philosophers, artists,
entrepreneurs and young people in order to distil the science
and stories behind our deepest struggles. Originally from
Bulgaria, she divides her time between London and Sofia.*

Late on a hot summer night six years ago, I found myself in a
room packed floor to ceiling with sweating bodies on bunk
beds. This was no prison or hippie commune, mind you. I had
just embarked on the Camino de Santiago – a gruelling
journey of 800 kilometres that starts from a small village in the
south of France, crosses northern Spain and ends ninety
kilometres from the Atlantic Ocean, in the town of Santiago
de Compostela. In medieval times the road to Santiago was a
major pilgrimage route that reached its finale at the town's

eponymous cathedral, which, according to legend, holds the remains of Saint James, one of Christ's apostles.

I am not religious but neither were most of the 200,000 people who would walk the camino that year. Unlike the ragged, world-weary, indulgence-seeking travellers of old, modern pilgrims come here clad in high-tech mountain gear and for reasons ranging from the lofty to the very, very prosaic. Among those I met at various points were: Catholics looking for divine communion; garden-variety spiritualists on the hunt for epiphanies and energy fields; hedge-fund managers in the throes of mid-life crises; recent graduates desperate to ward off adulthood for as long as they could; and a slew of curious, more practically motivated characters hoping for a soulmate, weight loss or cheap thrills.

As for me, what brought me to the camino that day in early June of 2012 was a sin I needed to atone for. At twenty-two, my track record of actual delinquency was laughable – unless you count a jaywalking fine I 'forgot' to pay or the ill-conceived attempts I'd made as a kid to get my younger sister disavowed by the family. And yet, I was convinced that what I had done was odious nonetheless, perhaps even irredeemable. True, no one was coming after me, few even knew about it and those who did, the ones who had suffered its consequences, saw it as an offshoot of my unnatural ambition. But I knew: somewhere I had gone horribly wrong and I doubted anything could fix it.

It was shortly after my university graduation. I had come out of academia inculcated with ideas that might have made for an easy *summa cum laude* but that, it was beginning to dawn on me, would not survive contact with the real world, which I was now hopelessly stuck in. I had spent the previous four years under the spell of science – acing abstract maths, devouring economics – but rather than enlightenment, it seemed I was in for a Greek tragedy: every pained effort to avoid the undesirable inevitably leading right into it.

The 'undesirable' being, of course, that confrontation between a feeble human mind and the hard questions of living. Science, with its beguiling premise that things make sense, was to me both an answer and an escape from answering. I relished the notion of a world governed by natural laws rather than one buffeted by sheer randomness. I took solace in thinking that the giant, unfathomable mess of existence had an inherent logic to it, that it could, in fact, be broken down, studied, distilled and contained by a clump of elegant equations.

The promise of an underlying order, some capital-T Truth, meant that all the helplessness of being a child and the strangeness of being a teen and the expectations of becoming a woman would eventually amount to something. Once, in English class, the professor asked us to write down our three deepest fears. I had no trouble coming up with a ranking:

1. Meaninglessness
2. Myself
3. Public speaking

Science quelled my existential angst with a mantra I clutched onto rabidly. It went something like this: anything that can be measured can be controlled; anything that can't be measured doesn't matter. It was a tantalising concept, that the world ticked with the soothing precision of a clockwork mechanism, and if I could figure out its fundamental calculus, I could do anything – not only parametrise hyperboloids but solve life as well.

It's here that things took a wrong turn and the seeds of sin were laid down. My newfound love of logic ran into my old and very desperate need for certainty, and I decided to take science out of the classroom and bring it to bear on my day-to-day life. In this I drew inspiration from several fields, but chiefly economics, which, despite its reputation, isn't (just) about prices and interest rates. To me, economics was a wondrous thing, a way of making decisions – from buying groceries to running a country – based on reason rather than sentiment and speculation. The curves and diagrams I crammed into my head married mathematical precision with practical reality – and that was precisely what I needed.

Emotion, after all, hadn't served me well. (At twenty-two, I could say this with a straight face I can neither muster nor afford today.) I always felt too strongly, loved too easily, dreamed too impossibly, thought too deeply, until I found myself at rock bottom or down some rabbit hole. Economics, on the other hand, stripped things down to a very simple, very sensible question – that of maximising a limited resource: my time. How to spend my time in the most optimal way – now that was a problem I could solve without plumbing the depths of my psyche and dealing with the ensuing emotional haemorrhage.

And so, from the second term of my freshman year, I turned into a model *Homo economicus* – the proverbial creature of cold rationality that draws decision trees and weighs the costs and benefits of every action and calculates the marginal utility of every hour spent doing one thing rather than another. This meant that nearly everything I used to do for pleasure alone was now an inefficient use of my time resource. Holing up with a cherished book at the end of the day was out of the question, and for a long time, I drifted off to sleep to the mammoth tomes of *Macroeconomics I* or *II* balanced on my sternum, their hard edges boring marks of crimson pink into my bony flesh.

Trips to the movies, once giddy adventures, turned into such guilt-ridden affairs that at one point I stopped going altogether. The opportunity cost was too high: in the two hours it'd take for the plot to unravel, I could've got all the way through Orwell's *1984* or a full chapter on line integrals. Then there was the tea party – part monthly ritual, part improvised therapy session my friends and I had concocted in our freshman year. We kept the name even though what normally transpired had none of the civility of an actual tea party and the occasion often featured red wine instead of tea. I remember many blissful Friday evenings, the four of us plonked down on a faded blue sofa in some distant corner of the dorm, counting woes, comparing miseries.

It always lifted my spirits, knowing that the others had it just as bad as I did, sometimes even worse. Suffering was glue, a badge of belonging. But then I stopped going to the tea parties. Long chats into the night simply didn't factor into my new mental calculus. For optimisation purposes, I told myself, it was necessary to stick to eight hours of unperturbed sleep, begun before midnight, when the marginal utility of each subsequent hour starts to drop.

No, I wasn't happy. Try to live like that – no hour wasted, no joule of energy unchannelled into some or other productive pursuit – and you end up losing your capacity to behold beauty. Not just to behold but also to bear it. I am reminded of the story of an American tourist in Eastern Europe who drove high up the mountains and the clean air so overpowered his lungs, clotted by big-city soot, it threw him into a violent coughing fit. He choked and rasped with pain, one arm clutched at his throat, the other grasping, blindly, for the car's exhaust pipe. I don't know if this really happened, but the image is seared into my memory: the man sucking on the pipe, inhaling fumes to keep himself alive, to stop clean air from reaching his lungs and killing him. When I heard this story as a kid, I rolled my eyes at these Americans and their spoiled American ways. But I see now how one's whole being can begin to reject that which is essential to life. Cold mountain air, just like anything deeply felt, can be too pure, too prickly, for those of us who've forged an existence on babyproof corners and soft edges.

For me back then, happiness was not the point anyway. Control was. And certainty. My chief motivation was to avoid the pain and disappointment of unmet expectations, an ambition fuelled not by desire to achieve but a fervent desperation not to fail. Fail what? I could never quite put my finger on it and yet failure was a constant presence. It was the thing that threatened to blow my cover, crack me open and put in front of me the questions that I knew were always there. Who am I? What am I doing? Where am I going? What is this all about?

I did forget these questions, for a while at least, thanks to the insulation from reality that academic life so readily provided. Science helped contrive a structure, construct a meaning, signpost experience and edit out the unexplainable bits. But once outside the halls of academia, that structure collapsed. The scaffolding that held up my illusions of control crumbled, fast. No sooner had I shed my graduation gown than a million mundanities I was ill-equipped to handle had to be handled.

Such as looking for a job. I harboured some vague notion of what that job would be – something significant, something that mattered – but there were no such jobs around that I could find. In my reality-distorting way, I saw myself as a kind of catcher-in-the-rye character, only instead of children I'd be catching countries in distress from my perch at the World Bank. I'd travel to places on the brink of poverty (or, more likely, in the thick of it) and pull them out of imminent collapse, a stack of economic papers in hand. It took the straight talk of several good and patient people to disabuse me of my Holden-esque vision, to let it sink in that things didn't work that way in the real world, that politics was always apt to mar the spotless theories of science.

There was also a father who had sacrificed his own ambitions for a family and a good name, and who expected the same of his daughter, me. Our conversations, until then few and far between, grew tense and urgent. When he talked about *job* and *family* and *house* and *prestige* – to him, the stuff of a life not wasted – the words got trapped in the air between us, hanging heavy in the wake of yet another argument, lingering long after it. Against the unimpeachable rectitude of Dad's words, my own aspirations looked perversely selfish and small.

I had no theory on hand to help me in this, no equation to solve for X. But more troubling to me was a nascent feeling that deep down I am a bad person. I watched as my few good friends drifted away, to families and new things, and watched, too, as the hallways in the dorms emptied out, people I'd seen but not really known walking past, lugging suitcases, saying goodbyes, their faces flashing in and out and away into the ether of the real world, and as I watched all this, I felt a sense of deserved abandonment. Did I, the self-proclaimed economist, really think that invulnerability would come free of charge? That by embracing the natural laws I could somehow transcend the human laws or skip altogether the lawlessness of being a person in the world?

In hindsight, I didn't go on the camino to find myself but to punish myself. That's partly the reason why I went into it utterly unprepared (also because I had no money). I took no guidebook (*The route markers better be good*, I thought), no hiking boots (*My sneakers better hold up*), no rain gear (*It better not rain*). I would've even left my phone behind if it weren't for the parents, who were told I was going on a month-long graduate school camp in Barcelona. (Every few days they'd call and I'd be sweating up a hill, and they'd ask about things and I'd give them my ready-made spiel: everything's good, Mum; we are studying Walmart's expansion strategy into Southeast Asia, Mum, and I'm just about to duck into class so really must go now, loveyoubye.)

Most of the time I just walked and walked and walked in silence. This wasn't always easy with so many people passing by and road etiquette demanding that you look up and greet them with a '*buen camino*' (literally 'good path' or 'have a safe trip'). I tried to wake up early and walk fast to avoid the conversations that here tend to pass over the small talk, going too deep too soon. I'd plod on in shorts and a T-shirt in the morning frost and the blistering afternoon sun, in the frequent drizzle and the occasional storm, for thirty to forty kilometres of often barren land, my feet soggy from Vaseline and cramped inside two layers of woollen socks.

I remember this one village where we were summoned to evening Mass. A beautiful old monastery built right in the centre, bells ringing, choir singing. As the other pilgrims flocked inside, I dithered out on the stone steps. I couldn't bring myself to go in; I didn't feel I belonged there. In my diary that night, I wrote sarcastically about all the churchiness one encounters on the road and how I just wanted to be left alone with my demons.

One sweltering afternoon about halfway on the camino, I arrived in a nondescript village called Molinaseca. At its far end were two small *albergues* (the pilgrim equivalent of hostels), and as I approached with the dozen or so other pilgrims, it was clear where everybody would be setting up camp for the night. New and shiny, made from light polished wood, the first *albergue* stood in stark contrast to the second one – a dingy building whose owner might as well have jumped straight out of a horror movie.

Dishevelled hair, wild eyes, one missing leg, the unmistakable smell of spirits on him, the ominous screeching noises of his plaster cast – everything spelled trouble. And yet, as my fellow travellers filed inside the new albergue, I felt strangely drawn to that other place. Every one of my instincts shouted danger, every shred of common sense rammed into my mind told me to stay away, but a strange compulsion overrode my better judgement. I stayed. The *hospitalero* bogeyman made me wait outside until his official opening time at one o'clock. I sat down on my backpack and fixed my eyes on the anorexic dog by my feet while the man played checkers with his pal, mumbling indistinctly under his breath. At one he let me in. Apparently, I was the only guest, although there were backpacks dropped on the dirty floor; I wondered what had happened to their owners. The whole place was dark and soaked with the musty tang of a ghost house. The light in the bathroom didn't work. The stairs creaked and I swallowed heavily as the man, leaning in the door frame, pointed upstairs.

Later outside he sat me down at the flimsy table and told me his life story – a story of love and a happy marriage, an accident that left him a cripple in his mid-twenties, the ensuing treachery of his wife, the heartbreak, the denial, the anger at God, the pilgrimage to Santiago, once, twice, thirteen times, until the demons had settled and he stayed in Molinaseca to shepherd other lunatics tangled in their own dramas. The man's name was Elisande, which, he reckoned, made us namesakes – people call me Ellie – and kindred spirits of sorts. I barely uttered a word the whole time he spoke and when his story ended, he stood up to bring some olive oil he'd made himself and wanted now to give to me, and as he made for the outhouse in the back, he looked over his shoulder and said, 'You are a good person, Ellie.' And just like that, they came unbidden, first belonging, then forgiveness, and in that moment it seemed to me that everything had stilled in its proper place.

A Very Long Walk
in a Very Cold Place

Ben Saunders

Ben Saunders is a record-breaking polar explorer who has covered more than 7,000 kilometres (4,350 miles) on foot in the polar regions. The third person in history to ski solo to the North and South Poles, Ben holds the record for the longest human-powered polar journey in history. He lives in the Cotswolds with his wife Pip and their labradoodle Molly.

It was just after Christmas 2013. I remember looking down at the wooden post – or perhaps it was a cardboard tube – in the middle of a patch of snow at the heart of a barren, deeply inhospitable continent and wondering who had painted the hand-drawn wonky red stripes that spiralled up it. For somewhere that had been so important to me for so much of my life, and that had caused me so much pain, I was surprised by how shoddy it looked. I was also surprised by my desire to get away as soon as we had arrived, not wanting to lose the momentum we had worked so hard to gain. It felt like the worst was behind us.

The South Pole is an odd spot. After standing there 101 years before Tarka and me, Captain Scott wrote in his diary, 'Great God! this is an awful place.' We were deep into Antarctica, home to the coldest, windiest, highest and driest land on the planet, an interminable white desert the size of India and China put together whose indigenous life – seals, penguins, terns, skuas and petrels – can only survive by the sea, on the continent's temperate outer fringes. The Pole itself is nearly a thousand miles from the coast and for a long time it represented the ultimate prize in the golden age of Edwardian exploration. Antarctica became the backdrop to many legendary stories. In early 1909, Sir Ernest Shackleton came within ninety-seven miles of the Pole before turning back ('I thought, dear, that you would rather have a live ass than a dead lion,' he later wrote to his wife). Captain Robert Scott's Terra Nova expedition reached the Pole on foot in January 1912 only to find that a Norwegian team, led by Roald Amundsen, riding on dog sleds and using skis, had beaten them to it. All five of Scott's team died on the trek home and for more than a century, his route to the South Pole and back remained unfinished, the high watermark of human endurance in the harshest climate on earth. To me, it was as if no one had broken the marathon record since 1912, and – for reasons not entirely clear to me at the time – completing this journey became an obsession that consumed much of my adult life.

*

My first polar expedition was in 2001. Veteran explorer Pen Hadow offered me the chance to join a small team that was setting out on foot from the north coast of Russia to the North Pole. I was twenty-three. I thought of the project as a one-off dream and never imagined it would morph into a career. The team eventually pulled out, leaving Pen and me two options: attempt the journey as a pair, or abandon the expedition and lose the sponsorship funds we had raised. On a shoestring budget and, in my case, with no experience of polar conditions, we suffered for fifty-nine days on the Arctic Ocean before quitting just over two-thirds of the way to the Pole. I came home crushed by the enormity of the challenge, but two years later returned to it, alone.

The 600-or-so-mile journey took me ten weeks. I never knew how far exactly I walked over the semi-frozen Arctic Ocean, my route wildly zigzagging to avoid open water and pressure ridges in the ice, always drifting under the colossal forces of the tides, the wind and the ocean currents. One day, after skiing north for nine gruelling hours, I ended up more than a mile south from where I'd started that morning. It was like trying to walk up the 'down' escalator and being unable to keep up.

I reached the North Pole on 11 May 2004. The moment was, in many ways, the ultimate anticlimax, mainly because there's nothing there. Not even a pole. Intellectually, of course, I understood that: with the sea ice forever shifting, breaking up and refreezing, there could never *be* anything permanent on the North Pole. But I still expected something to look different or, at least, feel different. The only way I knew I was at the top of the world was by counting down the numbers on my GPS. When they ticked over to 90 degrees, I sat down on my sledge, pulled out my satellite phone and dialled three numbers: my mum's, my girlfriend's and my sponsor's. I got three answerphones.

When my teammate Tarka l'Herpiniere and I turned our backs on the South Pole in December 2013 and began the return trip to the coast, I thought the hardest part of the expedition was over. With the wind at our backs, skiing downhill at times, all we had to do was retrace our steps, treading a path between the ten food caches we had buried on the outward journey. But as it turned out, the nothingness that stretched up ahead for 900 miles held something else in store.

For two months we had walked into a near-constant head-wind, so we assumed that after turning 180 degrees, the wind would blow at our backs. Then, two days later, it turned with us and we found ourselves yet again straining against it. In what should have been midsummer, we experienced some of the worst weather of the entire trip, each day slipping further behind our distance targets. We had reached the Pole in record time despite dragging heavier loads than anyone in history, but the energy that had carried us up the vast Beardmore Glacier, across the highest point of the Antarctic plateau and finally to the Pole itself was rapidly waning. Our sledges, 200 kilograms each at the beginning of the journey, were near-empty now but they still felt heavy. To eke out our dwindling food supplies, we ate half rations.

I felt shattered. My stomach developed a permanent growl, my ribs protruded, my legs buckled, my thoughts swam in fog. On our second day of half rations, I stopped in the middle of a storm to remove my outer jacket and add more insulating layers. I got dangerously cold and it was only because of Tarka, who zipped me up like a toddler while my arms hung useless by my side, that I stayed out of trouble. Compounding my physical decline was the self-admonishment going on in my head. How could I have miscalculated our rations? Why did I so wilfully ignore the experts who had warned me about the absurdity of this goal? Most of all, I berated myself for letting a vain, selfish pursuit put me and my friend in such extreme danger.

On New Year's Eve we woke up to the hardest of our 108 days in Antarctica, but in my state I didn't realise the gravity of the situation. The wind chill was −49 degrees Celsius when I recorded it, and we stayed outside for more than thirteen hours, on half the food I'd intended, wrapped in almost all the clothes we had. At rest breaks we ate halved energy bars and drank diluted energy drinks that tasted like lukewarm dishwater. Towards the ninth hour Tarka's familiar metronomic pace became erratic, and he seemed to stumble more than usual on ridges and divots in the snow surface. He stopped mid-session to remove his outer insulated vest, flipping back his hood as if he were too hot. From my experience leading polar expeditions, I recognised the telltale signs of hypothermia.

But I did not react. I was on the edge too, barely shuffling one foot in front of the other. All I can remember of that afternoon is how it slowly drifted into evening, the pale sun wheeling around us, the horizon erasing itself, then reappearing in a whirling fog of spindrift. I could think of nothing but the battle raging in my mind against the part of me that wanted so desperately to stop, to just lean my shoulders on the ski poles, slump forwards against the resistance of the sledge harness and rest, to hell with the consequences. At times I wondered what would happen if I fell over, whether I'd stand up again or find the energy to yell for Tarka, whether he'd even hear me over the noise of the wind.

I kept turning back to see Tarka, normally in my ski tracks and on my heels, fall further and further behind. I stopped a few times to let him catch up but it was too cold to wait for more than a minute before I started shivering, so I raised a single ski pole, he raised his in reply – a signal we often used – and I shuffled on. Looking over my shoulder, I watched him recede, the horizon sucking him backward, like quicksand. After a while he stopped raising his pole. I waited but by now he was a tiny dark speck in the white that took for ever to grow. I unclipped my harness and started to put up the tent, scrabbling to match the poles to their corresponding fabric sleeves, like a drunk taking some sort of coordination test. 'Sorry I'm late,' said Tarka when he arrived, but he sounded like someone else, his words mumbled and slow.

When we finished setting up camp, I saw him fumbling in his big outer mittens with the plastic buckles that strapped our sledges closed. 'I can't feel my hands,' he said through an ice-encrusted mask. As we zipped ourselves into the porch of the tent to take off our boots and outer layers before climbing into the sleeping bags, I noticed the tips of his thumbs. They were badly frost-nipped, if not entirely lost to frostbite. Fear washed over me, and anger – at him and at myself for letting this happen. I pulled up my jacket and two layers of fleece so he could warm his hands in my armpits. Thankfully, the colour and circulation started to return. We ate our half dinners in near silence and fell asleep exhausted and cold, knowing that in a few hours we'd have to live through this again.

Our first food cache was still forty-six miles away and all we had left was half a day's worth of supplies: eight energy bars, half a breakfast and half a dinner each. Ten miles into that day, Tarka slowed down again before stopping entirely and waving me over to talk. 'I feel really weak in the legs again,' he said. 'OK. What do you want to do about it?' I snapped back. It wasn't until a moment later that I realised: this was on me. Tarka had followed my lead towards a goal that many deemed impossible. For me, this was not just a dream; it was a responsibility too. I'd always imagined that conquering the Pole would be the single hardest thing I could ever do, but it turned out that the real crux was here, in this small moment, standing next to my friend, in a howling gale, miles away from anyone or anything, not knowing what to do.

It was reckless to continue like this, yet how could I give up now, so close to fulfilling the dream that had haunted me all this time? Admitting defeat felt like a waste – of so much effort, so many years of my life. Lying awake in my sleeping bag that night, I turned away from Tarka so he wouldn't see me cry. I felt bitterly disappointed but also ashamed at my disappointment, at the hubris that had brought us our current suffering. I ground my teeth as I struggled to make the decision that I had to make.

When I give talks and show photographs from my expeditions, the question I'm most often asked is why. What drove me to push myself so far and so hard for so many years? My well-polished answer is to talk about being 'an explorer of human limits rather than geographical limits' and about how I see myself as an unusual sort of athlete motivated by testing and extending my potential. This is not untrue, but it is also not entirely honest.

I can trace the roots of my extreme ambition to my father's disappearance when I was ten. He and my mother had been divorced for five years but my dad still visited us once or twice a month. He'd drive my brother and me back to his bedsit in Plymouth and take us to car-boot sales, fish and chips in front of Saturday-night TV or one of those dockyard working-men's clubs where his country band played. I don't recall the moment he vanished from our lives, but the visits stopped first, then the letters, then, finally, the birthday and Christmas cards.

I can't remember any conscious sense of loss or abandonment, although looking back now, it's clear that in my transition to manhood I found solace and guidance in the pages of *National Geographic* and books like Shackleton's

South!, Chris Bonington's *Everest the Hard Way* and Apsley Cherry-Garrard's *The Worst Journey in the World*. Reading them provided me with role models that now strike me as preposterous caricatures of macho accomplishment – all frozen beards, indomitable spirits, frostbitten digits and stiff upper lips. But to the eleven-year-old me, they filled the absence my father had left and served as a template for what it meant to be a man.

The final words of Tennyson's 'Ulysses' – 'To strive, to seek, to find, and not to yield' – are carved on what passes for Captain Scott's headstone, a simple wooden cross on Observation Hill in Antarctica, half a mile from where Tarka and I stooped to tighten our bootlaces at the start of our journey a century after Scott died in his tent from starvation, exhaustion and hypothermia. His 1910–12 Terra Nova expedition was officially undertaken in the name of science, and while the frozen notebook prised from the sleeping bag that became his burial shroud gives scant insight into his deepest motivation, I wonder if he and I were after something similar. Scott was twenty-nine when his father died, leaving him a business that soon went bankrupt, together with a widowed mother and two unmarried sisters to provide for from his modest Navy salary. Perhaps conquering Antarctica represented an achievement so profound it would not only lift Scott's family from poverty, but also quench that peculiar human desire for completion, resolution and wholeness that has dogged most of my adult life.

One of my closest friends is Buddhist and many years ago I wrote down something he'd mentioned in a conversation:

Dukkha. The first of Buddhism's Four Noble Truths, the term loosely translates as the pain and suffering – or rather, the 'unsatisfactoriness' – that pervades the human condition. I am not Buddhist, and for a long time I assumed that the proper response to Dukkha was simply to work harder. I thought that through ambition, application and persistence I would one day find happiness, inner peace and validation; that by striving, I'd make something of myself; and that if I could just pull my sledge to the South Pole and back, life would finally be OK.

After a fitful night in my sleeping bag, I decided not to call for evacuation but to request an airdrop of food so we could continue to our first cache. This would mean surrendering my goal to make the entire journey unsupported, but I had realised, at last, that our lives were not something I wanted to gamble with any longer. Up until now, we'd logged more than seventy hours of unrelenting physical exertion every week: twice as much as a Tour de France cyclist – and not over three weeks but ten. We had given it our all and we were lucky that neither of us had collapsed from exhaustion. And yet the day we spent lying and waiting for the aircraft was a dark one for both of us. Tarka seemed a broken man. 'It'll look like my fault,' he said, 'and that's a good thing for you.' The airdrop had cost us $100,000, the last bit of contingency in the sponsorship funds I'd raised, and the sum I had set aside in my mind as a reward for finishing the project. Spending it all now meant I'd get home broke, but I banished the thought: I'd figure that out when the time came.

The arrival of the little Twin Otter ski-plane was a strange moment. The pilot climbed down to hand us two bags of food – seven days' worth of expedition rations and a plastic bag of treats he must've scrambled together from the small base camp on the opposite side of Antarctica. He took off his glove to shake my hand and I did the same. Then, in the moment it took me to appreciate that this was the first time I'd touched the skin of another human being in ten weeks, he was gone. Tarka and I retreated to our sleeping bags and gorged ourselves for the rest of the day. That carrier bag was the greatest gift I had ever opened, full of what appeared to me exotic, alien delicacies: a homemade apple cake, a tube of Pringles, a tub of cream cheese, a packet of crackers and a mysteriously unfrozen bottle of Coca-Cola.

It took six more painful weeks to get to the finish line. The small crack in the ice between the jagged shore of Ross Island and the Ross Ice Shelf was a threshold I'd spent nearly two decades determined to cross one day, yet I'm not sure what I expected would happen when I stepped on the other side. All I remember about that moment of arrival is a vague feeling of relief, like an overly tight belt had finally been loosened. I think I held one ski pole up in the air, but only in response to a raised camera (a handful of New Zealand scientists had walked out to see us from a nearby base) and not from any sense of euphoria or triumph.

In the weeks and months that followed, life carried on much as it usually does, apart from the amounts of food I consumed. I struggled with the early media appearances and speaking commitments but they often came with the compensation of snacks or, if I was really lucky, free-for-all buffet breakfasts at fancy hotels. My appetite seemed to have lost its 'off' switch and I devoured anything on offer. It came to a point where I'd stand on stage talking about a pioneering feat of human endurance with a decent-sized paunch to show for it.

It took nine months to recover physically and perhaps the same time to overcome the ensuing sense of loss and emptiness. The force that had motivated me for years had evaporated. I felt as if a gravitational field had caught me in its orbit and kept me circling closer and closer, until my drive and work ethic and ambition all burned up on re-entry. Having finished what was arguably the most iconic polar expedition in history, it did not occur to me to congratulate myself. Instead, I searched the Queen's Birthday Honours list and New Year's Honours list for my name, secretly and in vain. The lack of significant public acclaim gave me all the ammunition I needed to berate myself for having fallen short somehow. Perhaps we hadn't achieved enough. Perhaps no one cared anyway.

Slowly, though, I began to think it was a mistake to assume that happiness would spring from the satisfaction of a grand desire, or that there was anything but the weakest of correlations between external validation and inner peace. I read the Norwegian explorer Erling Kagge, who referred to Antarctica as a very good school, and more than five years after stepping ashore at Ross Island, I am beginning to appreciate the subtler lessons of our very long walk in this very cold place.

The journey left me with a paradoxical belief: that the fulfilment of individual potential is one of the most important pursuits in life, yet genuine happiness (or perhaps peace is the better word) can only come from self-enquiry and self-acceptance. Striking the right balance between action and contemplation is a struggle we all share: how to imagine things as they could be while also accepting them as they are. For many years I thought that walking to the South Pole and back would be the sternest, most exacting task I could pit myself against. But traversing the plateaus of Antarctica was a simple thing compared to the inward journey that followed it.

I am no less ambitious today (I returned in 2017 to ski solo to the South Pole), but I've learned to see my goals as waypoints, not destinations. I've also realised that pinning your self-worth on external rewards is utterly futile because the more you accomplish, the more people you encounter whose achievements can make yours feel insignificant. When the mountaineer George Lowe, among the first to conquer Mount Everest, died in 2013, aged eighty-nine, one epitaph described him as a 'gentle soul,' and it struck me as perhaps the best thing I could aspire to. It's an aspiration with no finish line, a search that will last as long as life lasts. Ultimately, it's the expedition that beckons every one of us: to find meaning in the path we choose and the tracks we leave on our journeys, imperfect and never complete, and ours alone.

Further Reading and Resources

NB First publication date followed by an edition available now

A. J. Ashworth

A. J. Ashworth, *Somewhere Else, or Even Here* (Cromer: Salt Publishing, 2011)

Kate Leaver

Kate Leaver, *The Friendship Cure: Reconnecting in the Modern World* (London: Duckworth, 2019)

Susie Orbach, *Fat is a Feminist Issue*, with a new introduction (1978; London: Arrow, 2016)

Susie Orbach, *Hunger Strike: The Anorectic's Struggle as a Metaphor for Our Age* (1986; Abingdon: Routledge, 2018)

Irenosen Okojie

Clarissa Pinkola Estés, *Women Who Run with the Wolves: Contacting the Power of the Wild Woman* (1992; London: Rider, 2008)

Maggie Nelson, *Bluets* (London: Cape, 2017)

Cathy Rentzenbrink

Cathy Rentzenbrink, *The Last Act of Love: The Story of My Brother and His Sister* (London: Picador, 2015)

Cathy Rentzenbrink, *A Manual for Heartache: How to Feel Better* (London: Picador, 2017)

Ed Mitchell

Alcoholics Anonymous: https://www.alcoholics-anonymous. org.uk/

Ed Mitchell, *From Headlines to Hard Times* (London: John Blacke, 2009)

Saving Ed Mitchell (ITV documentary, 2008)

Emily Reynolds

Emily Reynolds, *A Beginner's Guide to Losing Your Mind: My Road to Staying Sane, and How to Navigate Yours* (London: Yellow Kite, 2018)

Hazel Gale

Hazel Gale, *The Mind Monster Solution: How to Overcome Self-sabotage and Reclaim Your Life* (London: Yellow Kite, 2018)

Lily Bailey

Lily Bailey, *Because We Are Bad: OCD and a Girl Lost in Thought* (Kindle edition: Canbury Press, 2016)

Rory Bremner

Rory Bremner, *ADHD and Me*, BBC2 documentary, 2017

Rory Bremner, 'A Lot of Mind-Wandering Goes On', teachwire, 2017

Rupert Hawksley, 'Rory Bremner: "Being officially diagnosed with ADHD in my fifties has been overwhelming"', *Daily Telegraph*, 21 April 2017

Ben Upton, 'An Interview with "Mr ACAMH" – Professor Eric Taylor', ACAMH, 2018

Jonathan Williams and Eric Taylor, 'The evolution of hyperactivity, impulsivity and cognitive diversity', *Journal of the Royal Society Interface*, 22 June 2006; 3(8): 399–413

Julian Baggini

Brené Brown, 'The Power of Vulnerability', *TED Talk*, June 2010

Arne Næss, *Ecology of Wisdom* (Penguin Classics, 2016)

Joe Shute, 'Wilko Johnson: "I knew I had survived cancer when my depression returned"', *Daily Telegraph*, 16 May 2016

Alex Christofi

Joan Didion, 'On Keeping a Notebook', in *Slouching Towards Bethlehem* (1968; New York, FSG Classics, 2008)

Selected Letters of Fyodor Dostoevsky. PG3328.A3 M27 (Rutgers University Press, c.1987)

Complete Letters of Fyodor Dostoevsky; ed. and trans. by David Lowe and Ronald Meyer (Ann Arbor, Mich.: Ardis, c.1988–1991, Volume 1)

Dostoevsky: Letters and Reminiscences, trans. by S. S. Koteliansky & J. Middleton Murry (London: Chatto & Windus, 1923)

Elitsa Dermendzhiyska

J. D. Salinger, *The Catcher in the Rye* (1951; London, Penguin, 2010)

Ben Saunders

Chris Bonington, *Everest the Hard Way* (1976; second-hand copies available)

Apsley Cherry-Garrard, *The Worst Journey in the World* (1922; London: Vintage, 2010)

David Crane, *Scott of the Antarctic: The Definitive Biography* (London: HarperPress, 2012)

Erling Kagge, *Philosophy for Polar Explorers* (2007; London: Viking, 2019)

Sir Ernest Shackleton, *South: The 'Endurance' Expedition* (1920; London: Penguin, 1999)

Sara Wheeler, *Terra Incognita: Travels in Antarctica* (New York: Modern Library, 1999)

Unbound is the world's first crowdfunding publisher, established in 2011.

We believe that wonderful things can happen when you clear a path for people who share a passion. That's why we've built a platform that brings together readers and authors to crowdfund books they believe in – and give fresh ideas that don't fit the traditional mould the chance they deserve.

This book is in your hands because readers made it possible. Everyone who pledged their support is listed below. Join them by visiting unbound.com and supporting a book today.

With thanks to patron, Brian Williamson, investor and entrepreneur, for his support:

I supported Ellie with this book firstly because she is fundamentally a good person. Secondly, mental health is like a hidden cancer in society, one we cannot bring ourselves to face for fear we uncover the reality of how many families it impacts. As a cancer survivor myself and with family members who have had mental health challenges, I know we need to normalise it through discussion and debate.

George Allen

Sandra Armor

Simona Atanasova

Sabra Attrill

Simone Baird

Maximilian Baker

Mariana Barakchieva

Amy Jane Barnes

Igor Barsi

Abigail Bereola

Lynne Blackwell

Gill Blow

Morven Bolam

Leo Bonnafous

Anna-Maria Bromley

Antony Brown

Brian Browne

Christine Burns

Hannah Cann

Isabel Cardoso

Tara Carlisle

Paul Child

Hannah Clegg

Kevin Conyers

Michael J Cook

Richard Cooper

Trenna Cormack

Ronald Cummings-John

Richard D'Souza

Eric Dacus

Ben Dare

Serena Davis

Harvey Day

Joyce de la Guerra

Tim Dedman

Ciaran Dickinson

Plamen Dimitrov

Dan Doran

Jonn Elledge

Andrew Evans

Anwen Evans

Nathan Filer

Vicky Folksman

Ruth Franklin

Tina Freeth

Sophie Gadd

Amy Gibson

Zsófia Ginter

Simon Graffy

Claire Grinham

Jacquelyn Guderley

Michael Guth

Gesche Haas

Charlotte Hakes

Josh Hall

Donna Hardcastle

Richard Harris

Andrew Harrison

Maximilian Hawker

Rich Hearn

Jo Higson

Sarah Hodsdon

Antonia Honeywell

Brett Hornby

Michael Horsley

Emmy Maddy Johnston

Sam Jones

Ella Kahn

Elie Katzenson

Dan Kieran

Don Krueger

Hoa La Vinh

Pete Lamb

Tamasin Little

Steve Loft

Nina Lomas

Patrícia Louro

Kavish M

Ian Mackintosh

Gabriel Mallows

Jimmy Manenski

Stefan Manov

Vivien Mast

Gail McAnena

Megan McCormick

Tom McTiernan

Jonny Miller

John Mitchinson

Carlo Navato

Michael Newsome

Dr John O'Hagan

Shona O'Keeffe

Gregory Olver

Kristann Orton

Jeremy Osborne

Kwaku Osei-Afrifa

Buki Papillon

Freya Partridge

Toby Pilditch

Simone Poggi

Justin Pollard

Sebastien Powell

Robert Reynolds

Sven Ripper

Jane Roberts

Lesley Robertson

Ben Robinson

Simon Roder

Bogs S

Tom Shacham

Evgeny Shadchnev

Laurence Shapiro

John Simmons

Stephanie Smith

Taylor Somerville

Dese'Rae Stage

Rory Stirling

Stoil Stoilov

Richard Taylor

Daniel Tenner

Chris Thompson

Sabine Tötemeyer

Deirdre Turner

David Tusek

Tony Vanderheyden

Richard Wallace

Helena Wasserman

Hannah Whelan

Cathy White

Andrew Whitehouse